Guitar Chord Songbook

Classic Rock

ISBN 978-0-634-06065-6

HAL•LEONARD®
CORPORATION

7777 W. BLUEMOUND RD. P.O. BOX 13819 MILWAUKEE, WI 53213

Visit Hal Leonard Online at
www.halleonard.com

Guitar Chord Songbook

Contents

Against the Wind

Words and Music
by Bob Seger

Melody:

It seems like yes-ter-day, __

G   Bm   C/G   D   Em   Am

Intro | G | | | |

Verse 1

G   Bm
It seems like yesterday,   but it was long ago.

C/G   G
Janey was lovely, she was the queen of my nights

D   C/G
There in the darkness with the radi-o playing low. And,

G   Bm
And the secrets that we shared,   the mountains that we moved.

C/G   G
Caught like a wildfire out of __ control

                    C/G   D
Till there was nothing left to burn and nothing left to prove.

Pre-Chorus 1

            Em   D   G
And I re-member what she said to me,

                      Em   C/G   G
How she swore ____ that it nev-er would end.

            Em   D   C/G
I re-member how she held ____ me, oh, ____ so tight.

                                    D
Wish I didn't know now what I didn't know then.

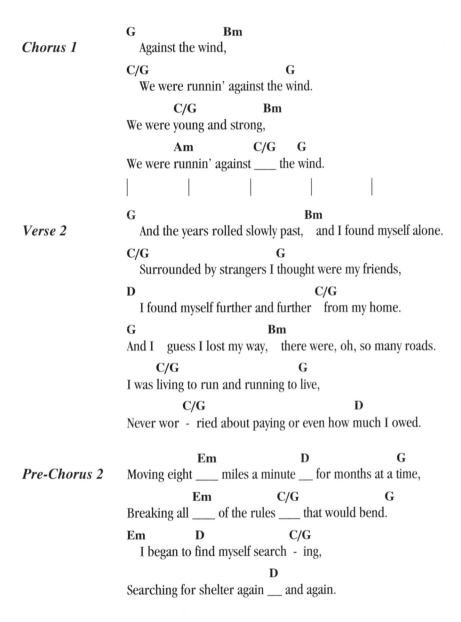

Chorus 1

G   Bm
  Against the wind,

C/G   G
  We were runnin' against the wind.

      C/G   Bm
We were young and strong,

      Am   C/G   G
We were runnin' against ___ the wind.

| | | | |

Verse 2

G   Bm
  And the years rolled slowly past, and I found myself alone.

C/G   G
  Surrounded by strangers I thought were my friends,

D   C/G
  I found myself further and further from my home.

G   Bm
And I   guess I lost my way, there were, oh, so many roads.

    C/G   G
I was living to run and running to live,

    C/G   D
Never wor - ried about paying or even how much I owed.

Pre-Chorus 2

      Em   D   G
Moving eight ___ miles a minute __ for months at a time,

      Em   C/G   G
Breaking all ___ of the rules ___ that would bend.

Em   D   C/G
  I began to find myself search - ing,

              D
Searching for shelter again __ and again.

Chorus 2

```
       G                    Bm
         Against the wind,

       C/G                          G
         Little something against the wind.

         C/G        Bm          Am          C/G     G
       I found myself ___ seeking shelter against ___ the wind.
       |         |          |          |          |
```

Piano Solo

```
| G        |        | Bm      |        |
| C/G      | G      | D       | C/G    |
| G        |        | Bm      |        |
| C/G      | G      | C/G     | D      |
```

Pre-Chorus 3

```
                Em          D          G
       Well, those drifter's days ___ are past me now,

                Em            C/G        G
       I've got so ___ much more to think about.

       Em     D          C/G
         Dead-lines and com-mitments,

                        D
       What to leave in,   what to leave out.
```

Chorus 3

```
       G                    Bm
         Against the wind,

       C/G                          G
         I'm still runnin' against the wind.

         C/G        Bm          Am          C/G     G
       I'm older now ___ but still runnin' against ___ the wind.

                    C/G     Bm          D                   C/G
       Well, I'm old - er now ___ and still runnin' against the wind.
```

Outro

```
                    G                C/G
       ||: Against the wind.  (Against the wind.)

                               G
       I'm still runnin'. ( Against the wind.)   :||  Repeat and fade
                                                      (w/voc. ad lib.)
```

All Along the Watchtower

Words and Music
by Bob Dylan

Tune down 1/2 step:
(low to high) E♭ –A♭ –D♭ –G♭ –B♭ –E♭

Melody:

There must be some kind a way out-ta here, ___

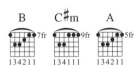

B   C#m   A

134211   134111   134211

Intro

B	C#m		B	A		B C#m		B	A
	B	C#m	B	A	B	
C#m	B	A	B	

Verse 1

C#m   B   A   B
    There must be some kind a way outta here,

C#m   B   A   B
    Say the jok-er to the thief.

C#m   B   A   B
    There's too much confusion,

C#m   B   A   B
    I can't get no re-lief.

C#m   B   A   B
    Business men, they, ah, drink my wine.

C#m   B   A   B
    Plow man, dig my earth.

C#m   B   A   B
    None will level on ___ the line,

C#m   B   A
    Nobody of it is worth. ___ Hey, hey!

| *Guitar Solo 1* | ‖: C#m | B | A | B | :‖ *Play 4 times* |

Verse 2	C#m	B	A	B
	No reason to get excit-ed,			

C#m   B   A B
The thief, he kindly spoke.

C#m   B   A B
There are man-y here among us

C#m   B   A B
Who feel that life ____ is but a joke.

   C#m   B   A
But, uh, but you and I, we've been ____ through that,

   B C#m   B   A B
But, ah, and this is not our fate.

C#m   B   A   B
So let us not talk false - ly now,

C#m   B   A   B
The hour's gettin' late, ____ ah. Hey!

| *Guitar Solo 2* | ‖: C#m | B | A | B | :‖ *Play 4 times* |

| *Interlude* | ‖: C#m | B | A | B | :‖ *Play 3 times* |
| | \| C#m | B | A | B | \| |

           Hey!

Guitar Solo 3 ‖: C#m   B |A   B   :‖ *Play 8 times*

Verse 3

      C#m B   A   B
Well, all a-long the watch - tower,

C#m   B   A   B
  Princes kept the view.

C#m   B   A   B
  While all the women came ___ and went,

C#m   B   A
  Bare feet servants too.

B   C#m B   A   B
  Well, ah, oh, outside in the cold distance, uh,

C#m   B   A   B
  A wild cat   did growl.

C#m   B   A   B
  Two riders were approachin'

       C#m B   A B
And the wind be-gan to howl.   Hey!

Outro ‖: C#m   B |A   B   :‖ *Repeat and fade*
(w/voc. ad lib.)

The Air That I Breathe

Words and Music by
Albert Hammond and Michael Hazelwood

(Capo 3rd fret)

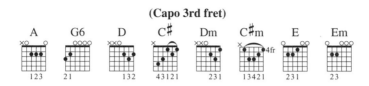

Intro | A | G6 | A | G6   D |

Verse 1

A   C#
If I could make a wish I think I'd pass;

D   Dm   A
Can't think of anything I need.

                              C#
No cigarettes, no sleep, no light, no sound,

D   Dm   A
Nothing to eat, no books to read.

C#m
Making love with you has left me

Dm   A
Peaceful, warm and tired.

C#m
What more could I ask,

             Dm   A
There's nothing left to be desired.

Pre-Chorus 1	**A** **C#**

A   **C#**

Pre-Chorus 1   Peace came upon me and it leaves me weak,

D   **Dm**   **A**

So sleep, silent angel, go to sleep.

A   **E**

Chorus 1   Sometimes all I need is the air ___ that I breathe,

        A   **E**

And to love you, all I need is the air ___ that I breathe.

        A   **E**

Yes, to love you, all I need is the air ___ that I breathe.

Guitar Solo 1   ‖: **Em** | **D** | **A** | **E**   :‖

Pre-Chorus 2   *Repeat Pre-Chorus 1*

Chorus 2   *Repeat Chorus 1*

Guitar Solo 2 | **Em** | **D** | **A** | **E** |

Chorus 3   *Repeat Chorus 1 till fade*

All Right Now

Words and Music by
Paul Rodgers and Andy Fraser

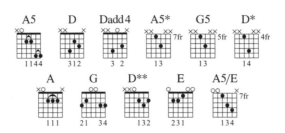

A5 D Dadd4 A5* G5 D*

A G D** E A5/E

Intro

| A5   D | A5 | Dadd4   D | A5 |
                                         Whoa.

| A5   D | A5 | Dadd4   D | A5 |
Ow!

Verse 1

          A5   D A5
There she stood in the street,

    Dadd4   D   A5
Smil - in' from her head to her feet.

                         D A5
I said a, "Hey, now, what is this?

                    Dadd4   D   A5
Now, baby, maybe, may - be she's in need of a kiss."

                  D   A5
I said a, "Hey, uh-huh, what's your name, baby?

    Dadd4   D   A5
May - be we can see things the same.

                  D A5
Now don't you wait or ____ hesitate.

    Dadd4   D   A5
Let's move ____ before they raise the parking rate." Ow!

GUITAR CHORD SONGBOOK

                    A5*   G5   D*   A5*
Chorus 1   All right ___ now. Baby, it's all ___ right now.

                           G5   D*   A5*
                    All right ___ now. Baby, it's all ___ right now, ___ woh.

                    A5   D   A5   Dadd4 D   A5
                       Let me tell ya now.   Oo, ah.

                                    A5   D   A5
Verse 2   I took her home ___ to my place,

                          Dadd4   D   A5
                    Watch - in' ev'ry move on her face.

                                           D   A5
                    She said, "Look, what's your game, baby?

                          Dadd4   D   A5
                    Are ___ you try'n' to put me in shame?"

                                           D   A5
                    I said a, "Slow, don't go so fast.

                          Dadd4   D   A5
                    Don't ___ you think that love can last?"

                                           D   A5
                    She said, "Love? Lord ___ a-bove.

                          Dadd4   D   A5
                    Oo. Now ___ you're try'n' to trick me in love." Ow!

                    A5*   G5   D*   A5*
Chorus 2   All right ___ now. Baby, it's all ___ right now.

                           G5   D*   A5*
                    All right ___ now. Baby, it's all ___ right now.

                    Yeah, it's all right now.

Guitar Solo 1 | A | | | |
                    | | | | |

Interlude | A   . | G   D** | A   . | G   D* |

Guitar Solo 2   ‖: A | G   D**   :‖ *Play 16 times*
| E | |
Oh, yeah.

Bridge

A5   D/A A5   Dadd4   D
Ow!

A5
Let me tell you all about it now.

D/A   A5   Dadd4   D   A5
Ow!   Yeah.

Verse 3   *Repeat Verse 2*

Chorus 3

A5*   G5   D*   A5*
All right ____ now. Baby, it's all ____ right now.

G5   D*   A5*
All right ____ now. Baby, it's all ____ right now.

Outro

A5*   G5   D*   A5*
All right now. Baby, it's all ____   right.

G5
Yeah, all right now.

D*   A5*
Baby, baby, baby, it's all right.

G5
All, all right now. Yeah.

D*   A5*
It's all right, it's all right, it's all right, yeah, huh.

G5   D*   A5*
All right now. Baby, it's all ____ right now.

G5
Yeah, we're so happy together. Ow!

D*   A5*
It's all right, it's all right, it's all right.

G5   D*   A5/E
Ev'rything's all right. Yeah.   Woo!

Authority Song

Words and Music by
John Mellencamp

Drop D tuning:
(low to high) D–A–D–G–B–E

Melody:

They __ like to get you in a

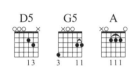

D5 G5 A

Intro

| N.C. | | |

‖: D5 | | | :‖

Verse 1

      D5   G5   A   D5   G5   A
They __ like to get you in a compro-mising po-sition.

            D5   G5
Yeah, they __ like to get you there

        A   D5   G5   A
And smile __ in your face.

        D5
Yeah, they think they're so cute

        G5   A   D5   G5   A
When they got you in that con-dition.

  D5   G5 A   D5   G5   A
But I think it's a to - tal dis-grace. And __ I say,

Chorus 1

  D5   G5   A   D5   G5   A
I fight authority, au-thority always wins.

  D5   G5   A   D5   G5   A
Well, I fight authority, au-thority always wins.

           D5   G5
Well, I've been doing it since I was a young kid

    A   D5   G5 A
And I come out grinning.

        D5   G5   A   D5 G5   A
Well, I __ fight authority, au-thority always wins.   Oh, yeah.

Interlude 1   ‖: D5 | G5 A   :‖

Verse 2
```
                  D5                          G5
              I call up my preacher, I say,

                      A               D5          G5    A
              "Give me strength for round __ five."

                  D5                          G5
              He said, "You don't need no strength,

                      A          D5     G5   A
              You need to grow up, son."

                  D5                     G5          A       D5     G5   A
              I said, "Growing up leads to grow  -  ing old and then to dying.

                  D5                     G5       A              D5
              Ooh, and dying to me don't sound ____ like all that much fun."

                  G5  A
              And so I say,
```

Chorus 2
```
              D5              G5    A    D5      G5   A
              I fight authority, au-thority always wins.

                      D5              G5    A    D5      G5  A
              Well, I __ fight authority, au-thority always wins.

                          D5                     G5
              Well, I've been doing it since I was a young kid;

              A          D5       G5   A
              I've come out grinning.

                      D5                  G5    A    D5      G5   A
              Well, I __ fight authority, au-thority always wins.
```

| *Guitar Solo* | ‖:D5   \|G5 A   :‖   *Play 8 times* |

N.C.

Interlude 2   I say oh, ___ no, no, no.

I say oh, no, no, no.

I say oh, no, no, no, no.

N.C.

Chorus 3   I fight authority, authority always wins.

I fight authority, authority always wins. Kick it in.

         D5   **G5**

I've been doing it since I was a young kid

        A   **D5**   **G5** **A**

And I've come out grinning.

        D5

Outro   Well, I ___ fight authority,

    G5   **A**   **D5**   **G5**   **A**

Au-thority always wins.

        D5

‖: Well, I ___ fight authority,

    G5   **A**   **D5**   **G5**   **A**

Au-thority always wins.   :‖ *Repeat and fade*

All the Young Dudes

Words and Music
by David Bowie

Melody:

Bil - ly rapped all night a - bout his su - i - cide, _ how he'd

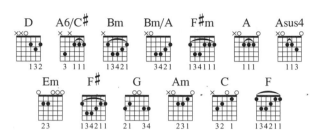

D A6/C♯ Bm Bm/A F♯m A Asus4
Em F♯ G Am C F

Intro |D A6/C♯ |Bm Bm/A |F♯m |A |

Verse 1

      D   **A6/C♯**
Billy rapped all night about his suicide,

          Bm   **Bm/A**
How he'd kick it in the head when he reached twenty-five.

F♯m   **A**
    That speed jive. Don't wanna stay alive __ when you're twenty-five.

D   **A6/C♯**
Wendy's stealing clothes from marks and sparks,

Bm   **Bm/A**   **F♯m**
And Freddy's got spots from ripping off stars from his face.

             A   **Asus4**
A funky little boat race.

      Em
The television man is crazy,

      F♯   **Bm**   **Bm/A**
Saying we're juvenile delinquent wrecks.

G   **D**   **A**
Man, I need a T.V. ___ when I've got T. Rex.

Hey, mister, you guessed, I'm a dude, dad.

Chorus 1

    D A6/C#   Bm Bm/A   Am
    All the young dudes _____ carry the news.

C   F C   G   C   A
Boogaloo dudes __ carry the news.

    D A6/C#   Bm Bm/A   Am
    All the young dudes _____ carry the news.

C   F C   G   C   A
Boogaloo dudes __ carry the news.

Verse 2

       D   A6/C#
Now Lucy looks sweet 'cause he dresses like a queen,

     Bm   Bm/A
But he can kick like a mule, it's a real mean team.

     F#m   A
But we can love, oh, we got love.

D   A6/C#
Brother's back at home with his Beatles and his Stones.

    Bm   Bm/A
We never got it off on this revolution stuff.

F#m   A   Asus4
   What a drag, too many snags.

Em
Drunk a lot of wine and I'm feeling fine.

    F#   Bm Bm/A
Gotta race some cat to bed.

       G   D   A
Is there concrete all a-round or in my head?

Just in my head? Yeah, I'm a dude, dad.

Chorus 2   *Repeat Chorus 1*

Outro

    D A6/C#   Bm Bm/A   Am
‖: All the young dudes _____ carry the news.

C   F C   G C A
Boogaloo dudes __ carry the news.   :‖ ***Repeat and fade***

American Girl

Words and Music
by Tom Petty

Melody:

Well, she was an A - mer - i - can girl

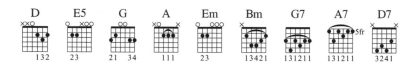

D   E5   G   A   Em   Bm   G7   A7   D7

Intro

‖: **D** | | | :‖

‖: **D** | **E5** | **G** | **A** :‖

Verse 1

  D   **E5**
  Well, she was an A-merican girl

G   **A**
  Raised on promises.

D   **E5**
  She couldn't help thinkin'

               G   **A**
That there was a little more to life somewhere else.

              D
After all it was a great big world

G   **Em**
  With lots of places to run to.

A
Yeah, and if she had to die tryin' she

Had one little promise she was gonna keep.

Chorus 1

G   A
Oh, yeah,   all right.

D
Take it easy, baby,

Bm
Make it last all night.

G   A   D
She was   an American girl.

Verse 2

D   E5
Well, it was kind of cold that night.

G   A
She stood all alone over the balcony.

D   E5
Yeah, she could hear the cars roll by

        G   A
Out on 441 like waves crashin' on the beach.

                         D
And for one desperate moment there,

G   Em
He crept back in her memory.

A
God, it's so painful when somethin' that is so close

Is still so far out of reach.

Chorus 2   *Repeat Chorus 1*

Interlude   ‖: G7 | A7 D7 :‖ *Play 3 times*
              | G7 | A7 |
              | D | | | |
              | | E5 | G | A |
              | D | E5 | G | A |

Outro   ‖: D | E5 | G | A   :‖ *Repeat and fade*

Badge

Words and Music by
Eric Clapton and George Harrison

Melody:

Think-in' 'bout the times you drove _ in my car. ___

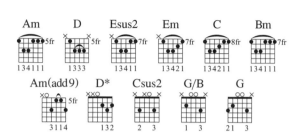

Am D Esus2 Em C Bm
Am(add9) D* Csus2 G/B G

Intro |Am |D |Am |D |

Verse 1

Am   D   Esus2 Em
    Thinkin' 'bout the times you drove in my car.

Am   D   Esus2 Em
    Thinkin' that I might have drove you too far.

C   Am   Bm Am(add9)
    And I'm thinkin' 'bout the love that you made on my ta - ble.

Verse 2

Am   D   Esus2 Em
    I told you not to wander 'round in the dark.

Am   D   Esus2 Em
    I told you 'bout the swans, that they live in the park.

C   Am   Bm Am(add9)
    Then I told you 'bout our kid, now he's married to Ma - ble.

Interlude | **D*** **Csus2**| **G/B** **G** |**D*** **Csus2**| **G/B** **G**|

Bridge

    D*   **Csus2**   **G/B** **G** **D***
Yes, I told you that the light goes up and down.

      Csus2   **G/B**   **G**   **D***
Don't you notice how the wheel goes 'round?

      Csus2   **G/B**   **G** **D***
And you better pick yourself up from the ground

   Csus2   **G/B**   **G**   **D***
Be-fore they bring the cur-tain down.

      Csus2   **G/B**   **G**   **D***
Yes, be-fore they bring the cur-tain down.

Guitar Solo | **D***   **Csus2**| **G/B**   **G** |

               ||:**D***   **Csus2**| **G/B**   **G** :|| *Play 6 times*

               | **D** |

Verse 3

  Am   **D**   **Esus2** **Em**
Talkin' 'bout a girl that looks quite like you.

  Am   **D**   **Esus2** **Em**
She didn't have the time to wait in the queue.

  C   **Am**   **Bm** **Am(add9)**
She cried away her life since she fell off the cra - dle.

Bang a Gong
(Get It On)

Words and Music
by Marc Bolan

Melody:

Well, you're dirt - y and sweet,

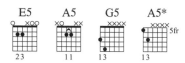

E5   A5   G5   A5*

2 3	1 1	1 3	1 3

Intro   ‖: E5 | | | :‖

Verse 1
                   E5   **A5**
Well, you're dirt - y and sweet, clad in black,

                   E5
Don't look back, and I love __ you.

    A5   **E5**
You're dirty and sweet, oh yeah.

Well, you're slim and you're weak,

              A5   **E5**
You've got the teeth of the hydra upon __ you.

    A5   **E5**
You're dirty, sweet and you're my girl.

Chorus 1
            G5   **A5***   **E5**
Get it on. ____ Bang a gong. ____ Get it on.

            G5   **A5***   **E5**
Get it on. ____ Bang a gong. ____ Get it on.

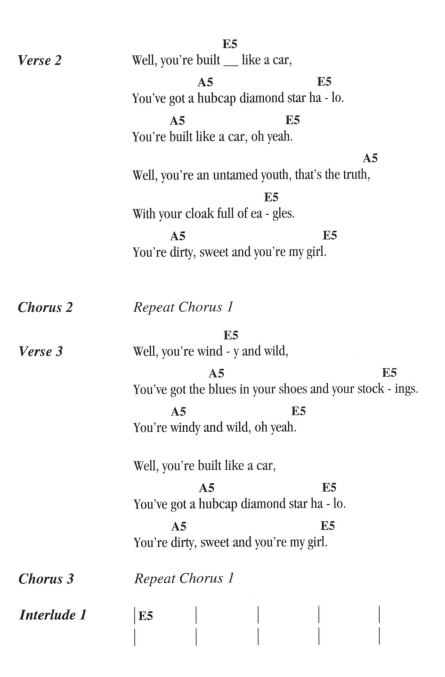

Verse 2

E5
Well, you're built __ like a car,

A5   E5
You've got a hubcap diamond star ha - lo.

A5   E5
You're built like a car, oh yeah.

A5
Well, you're an untamed youth, that's the truth,

E5
With your cloak full of ea - gles.

A5   E5
You're dirty, sweet and you're my girl.

Chorus 2   *Repeat Chorus 1*

Verse 3

E5
Well, you're wind - y and wild,

A5   E5
You've got the blues in your shoes and your stock - ings.

A5   E5
You're windy and wild, oh yeah.

Well, you're built like a car,

A5   E5
You've got a hubcap diamond star ha - lo.

A5   E5
You're dirty, sweet and you're my girl.

Chorus 3   *Repeat Chorus 1*

Interlude 1 | E5 | | | |
                        | | | | |

		E5

Verse 4

               E5
Well, you're dirt - y and sweet, clad in black,
A5   **E5**
  Don't look back and I love __ you.
     A5   **E5**
You're dirty and sweet, oh yeah.

Well, you dance when you walk,
       A5   **E5**
So let's dance, ____ take a chance, understand ____ me.
   A5   **E5**
You're dirty, sweet and you're my girl.

Chorus 4

          G5   **A5***   **E5**
Get it on. ____ Bang a gong. ____ Get it on.
          G5   **A5***   **E5**
Get it on. ____ Bang a gong. ____ Get it on.   Ow!
          G5   **A5***   **E5**
Get it on. ____ Bang a gong. ____ Get it on.   Ow!

Interlude 2

E5				

Sax Solo

E5				

Chorus 5

          G5   **A5***
Get it on. ____ Bang a gong. ____ Get it on.
E5
  Uh, uh, uh, uh, uh, uh.
          G5   **A5***
Get it on. ____ Bang a gong. ____ Get it on.
E5
  Uh, uh, uh, uh, uh.
          G5   **A5***
Get it on. ____ Bang a gong. ____ Get it on.
E5
  Uh, uh, uh, uh, uh, uh.
          G5   **A5***   **E5**
Get it on. ____ Bang a gong. ____ Get it on.   *Take me.*

Outro

G5	**A5***	**E5**		
‖: **E5**		:‖ *Repeat and fade*		

Call Me

from the Paramount Motion Picture
AMERICAN GIGOLO

Words by Deborah Harry
Music by Giorgio Moroder

Melody:

Col-or me ___ your col - or, ba - by.

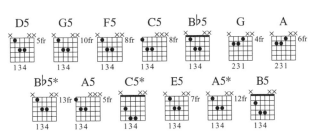

D5   G5   F5   C5   Bb5   G   A

Bb5*   A5   C5*   E5   A5*   B5

Intro   ‖: D5 | G5 F5 | D5 | F5 C5 :‖

Verse 1

D5
Color me your color, baby.

Bb5
Color me your car.

D5
Color me your color, darlin'.

Bb5
I know who you are.

Pre-Chorus 1

G   A
Come up off your col - or chart.

G   A
I know where you're com - ing from.

Chorus 1

        D5   F5
Call me ___ (Call me.) on the line.

        G5   Bb5*
Call me. Call me any, anytime.

        D5   F5
Call me. ___ (Call me.) I'll arrive.

        G5   Bb5*   N.C.   D5
You can call me any day ___ or ___ night. Call me.

Interlude 1	|**D5** | **G5 F5** |**D5** | **F5 C5**|	

Verse 2

D5
Cover me with kisses, baby.

B♭5
Cover me with love.

D5
Roll me in designer sheets,

  B♭5
I'll never get enough.

Pre-Chorus 2

  G   **A**
E-motions come, I don't __ know why.

G   **A**
Cover up love's alibi.

Chorus 2

C5*   **D5**   **F5**
Call me ___ (Call me.) on the line.

     G5   **B♭5**
Call me. Call me any, anytime.

    D5   **F5**
Call me. ___ (Call me.) I'll arrive.

     G5   **B♭5** N.C.
When you're ready we can share the wine.

   D5
Call me.

Interlude 2 | D5 | G5 F5 | E5 | A5* G5 |

Bridge
    E5   B5
    Oo, he speaks the lan - guages of love.

    E5   B5
    Oo, amore le chia - mami.   *Chiamami.*

    F5   C5
    Oo, appelle moi mon cherie.   *Appelle moi.*

               D5   Bb5
    Anytime, ___ anyplace, anywhere, anyway.

               G5   A5
    Anytime, ___ anyplace, anywhere, any day, anyway.

Synth Solo ||: E5 | | B5 | | :||
                | F5 | | C5 | | |
                | D5 | | Bb5 | | |
                | G5 | | A5 | | |

Chorus 3
    C5   D5   F5
    Call me, ___ (Call me.) my love.

               G5   Bb5
    Call me. Call me any, anytime.

Outro
          D5   F5
    ||: Call me (Call me.) for a ride.

          G5   Bb5
    Call me. Call me for some overtime.   :|| ***Repeat and fade***
                                                    (w/voc. ad lib.)

Bat Out of Hell

Words and Music
by Jim Steinman

Melody:

The si - rens are scream - ing and the

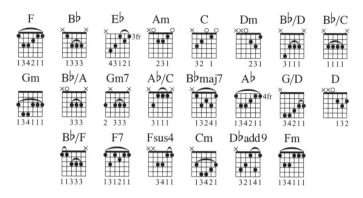

Intro   ‖: F | Bb Eb :‖

Verse 1

      F   **Bb**
The sirens are screaming and the fires are howling

    F
Way down in the valley tonight.

Eb   **F**   **Am**
There's a man in the shadows with a gun in his eye,

      Bb
And a blade shining, oh, so bright.

        F   **C**
There's evil in the air and there's thun - der in the sky,

     Dm   **C** **Bb**
And a killer's on the blood-shot streets.

      F   **C**
And down in the tunnel where the deadly are rising,

     Dm   **Bb/D**
Oh, I swear I saw a young boy down in the gutter,

                     C **Bb/C** **C**
He was starting to foam in the heat.

Pre-Chorus 1

    B♭   C
Oh, baby, you're the only thing in this whole world

       F   B♭
That's pure and good and right.

                                 C
And wherever you are, and wher-ever you go,

       B♭   C   F
There's always gonna be some light.

      B♭   C
But I gotta get out, I gotta break it out now,

    Dm   B♭
Be-fore the final crack of dawn.

      F   C
So we gotta make the most of our one night together,

        B♭   C   B♭/C   C
When it's over you know, we'll both be so alone.

Chorus 1

        F
Like a bat out of hell,

          B♭   F
I'll be gone ___ when the morning comes.

                       Am
When the night is over, like a bat out of hell,

     B♭ Am Gm
I'll be gone, gone, gone.

     F
Like a bat out of hell,

            C   B♭
I'll be gone ___ when the morning comes.

C B♭ C   F   C
    But when the day is done and the sun goes down,

       B♭   Gm Am B♭
And the moonlight's shining through,

C   F   Am   Dm   F
   Then like a sinner be-fore the gates of heaven,

     B♭   B♭/A Gm7   B♭   C   B♭   C
I'll come crawling on back to you.

Verse 2

    F   Bb
I'm gonna hit the highway like a battering ram

    F
On a silver black phantom bike.

                      Am
When the metal is hot and the engine is hungry,

        Bb
And we're all about to see the light.

F   C
Nothing ever grows in this rotting old hole,

    Dm   Bb
And everything is stunted and lost.

     F   C
And nothing really rocks and noth - ing really rolls,

      Bb   C   F
And noth - ing's ever worth the cost.

      Bb   C   F
And I know that I'm damned ___ if I never get out,

      Bb   C   F
And maybe I'm damned ___ if I do.

        Bb   C   Dm
But with ev - 'ry other beat I got left in my heart,

        Bb   C   F
You know I'd rather be damned ___ with you.

                      C
If I gotta be damned, you know, I wanna be damned,

Bb   C   F
Dancing through the night with you.

                    C
If I gotta be damned, you know, I wanna be damned,

F   Bb
Gotta be damned, you know I wanna be damned,

F   C
Gotta be damned, you know I wanna be damned,

Bb   C Bb   C
Dancing through the night, dancing through the night,

Bb   C   F
Dancing through the night with you.

| *Interlude 1* | F | | | E♭ | B♭/D A♭/C |
| | F E♭ | B♭/D A♭/C C | | |

Pre-Chorus 2   *Repeat Pre-Chorus 1*

Chorus 2

     F
Like a bat out of hell,

          B♭   **F**
I'll be gone ____ when the morning comes.

                   Am
When the night is over, like a bat out of hell,

      B♭   **Am**   **Gm**
I'll be gone, gone, gone.

      F
Like a bat out of hell,

          C   **B♭**
I'll be gone ____ when the morning comes.

C B♭ C   **F**   **C**
   But when the day is done and the sun goes down,

       B♭   **Gm Am B♭**
And the moonlight's shining through,

C   **F**   **Am**   **Dm**   **F**
  Then like a sinner be-fore the gates of heaven,

      B♭maj7   **B♭/A** **Gm7**
I'll come crawling on back to you.

         F   **Am**   **Dm**   **F**
Then like a sinner be-fore the gates of heaven,

      B♭   **B♭/A** **Gm7**
I'll come crawling on back to you.

Interlude 2 | F | | Ab | |
                    | Eb | | C | |
                    | G/D | D | G/D | D |
                    | Bb/F | F | Bb/F | F |

Verse 3

                             Bb
I can see myself tearing up the road,

     Eb Bb   **Eb Bb Eb Bb**   **F**   **F7**
Fast-er than any other boy has ev - er gone.

           Bb   **Eb**   **Bb**
And my skin is raw but my soul is ripe,

And no one's gonna stop me now,

                        F
I'm gonna make my es-cape!

      Eb   **Bb**   **F**
But I can't stop thinking of you,

      Ab   **Eb**
And I never see the sudden curve

                  Fsus4   **F**
Till it's way too late.

 | C | Bb F Gm7 | F   C |
Bb **F** **Gm7** **Ab**   **Eb**
          And I never see the sudden curve

                F
Till it's way too late.

Verse 4

       E♭   **F**   **Gm**
Then I'm dying at the bottom of the pit in the blazing sun.

E♭   **F**   **Gm**
Torn and twisted at the foot of a burning bike.

     A♭   **B♭**   **Cm**
And I think somebody some-where must be tolling a bell.

      E♭   **F**   **Gm**   **E♭**
And the last thing I see is my heart still beating.

      Gm   **Cm**
Breaking out of my body and flying away,

C   **Fsus4** **F**
  Like a bat out of hell!

     A♭   **B♭**   **Cm**
Then I'm dying at the bottom of a pit in the blazing sun.

A♭   **B♭**   **Cm**
Torn and twisted at the foot of a burning bike.

     E♭   **F**   **Gm**
And I think somebody some-where must be tolling a bell.

     A♭   **B♭**   **Cm**
And the last thing I see is my heart,

    D♭add9
Still beating, still beating,

      Fm   **C**
Breaking out of my body and flying away

Outro

N.C.   **F** **C**
Like a bat out of hell!

B♭   **F** **C**
  Like a bat out of hell!

B♭   **F**   **Fm**
  Like a bat out of hell!

C   **F**   **C**   **B♭**
  Like a bat out of hell!

       F   **C**   **B♭**
Like a bat out of hell!

    C   **F**   **C**   **F**
Like a bat out of hell!

Beast of Burden

Words and Music by
Mick Jagger and Keith Richards

Melody:

I'll nev-er be __ your beast __ of bur-den.

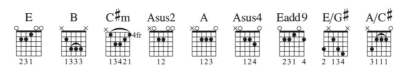

E   B   C#m   Asus2   A   Asus4   Eadd9   E/G#   A/C#

Intro
E B C#m	Asus2 B	E B C#m
Asus2 A B	E B C#m	A B E
B C#m	Asus2 B

Verse 1

E   B   C#m   A   B
I'll never be ____ your beast of burden.

E   B   C#m   Asus2 A B
My back is broad, ____   but it's a hurt - in'.

E   B C#m   A   E   B   C#m   Asus2 A B
All I want   for you to make a love to me.

Verse 2

E   B   C#m   A   B
I'll never be ____ your beast of burden.

E   B C#m   A   E
I've walked for miles, ____   my feet are hurtin'.

E   B   C#m   A   E   B   C#m   Asus2
All I want for you to make a love to me.

Chorus 1

A   Asus4   A
Am I hard e   -   nough?

            Eadd9   E
Am I rough e   -   nough?

        A
Am I rich enough?

        E   B   E/G# B
I'm not too blind to see.

Verse 3

```
E              B  C#m          A    B E
I'll never be ____ your beast of bur - den,
              B  C#m      E  A/C#     B
So let's go home       and draw the curtains, uh.
E             B  C#m
Music on the ra-dio,    come on, baby,
   A/C#  B           E B  C#m   Asus2 A
Make sweet  love to me, ____ yeah.
```

Chorus 2

```
         Asus4   A
Am I hard ____ e - nough?

   E      Eadd9
Am I rough enough?

   A
Am I rich enough?

   E              B  E/G# B
I'm not too blind to see.


Oh, little sister.
```

Guitar Solo

```
| E        B  C#m |      Asus2  A    B |
 (Pretty, pret-ty,        pretty, pret - ty girls.)
||: E       B  C#m |      Asus2  A    B :||
| E         B  C#m |      Asus2  A    B |
```

Interlude

```
E              B    C#m       Asus2 A  B
Pretty, pretty, pret-ty, pret-ty, pretty, pret-ty,     girl.
E              B    C#m       Asus2 A  B
Pretty, pretty, such a pret-ty , pretty, pret-ty      girl.
E         B  C#m Asus2 A  B   E  B  C#m
Come on, ba-by, please, please,    please.
```

Verse 4

```
              Asus2  A      B
I tell ya,          you can

E        B   C#m  Asus2  A      B
Put me out       on the       street,

E        B                C#m    Asus2  A
Put me out with no shoes ___ on my feet,

B   E          B      C#m
But put me out, put me out,

            Asus2  A   B   E    B  C#m  Asus2  A   B
Put me out of       miser-y. ___ 'Eah.
```

Verse 5

```
E                C#m          Asus2  A   E
All your sickness, I can suck it up.

E          B   C#m          Asus2  A
Throw it all at me,    I'll just shrug it off.

E          B   C#m         Asus2  A
There's one thing, baby,   I don't un-derstand:

E              B      C#m           Asus2  A
  You keep on tell-in' me I ain't your kind of      man.
```

Chorus 3

```
   B   E          B    C#m      Asus2  A
Ain't I  rough enough? Oo, ___ honey.

   B   E           B  C#m  Asus2  A
Ain't I  tough enough?

   B   E           B      C#m
Ain't I  rich enough? In love enough?

Asus2  A  B   E    B  C#m  Asus2  A   B
Oo,     oo, please.
```

Outro

```
E            B  C#m        Asus2  A      B
   I'll never be ___ your beast of bur    -   den.

E            B  C#m         Asus2  A      B
   I'll never be ___ your beast of bur    -   den.

E            B      C#m
Never, never, nev-er, nev-er,

           Asus2  A    B  E  B   C#m
Never, nev-er,     never be.____

     Asus2  A  B
Shh.

E            B  C#m        Asus2  A      B
   I'll never be    your beast of bur    -  den.

E                  B   C#m
   I've walked for miles,

      Asus2  A         E
My feet are     hurtin', uh.

        B       C#m        Asus2
Well, all I want is you to make

A    E    B  C#m  A  E
Love to me. Uh.     Yeah.

           B  C#m      Asus2  A          E
  I don't need    no beast of bur    -   den, uh.

           B  C#m   A        B
I need no fus-sin'. I need no nursin'.

     E          B       C#m
Nev-er, never, nev-er, nev-er,

           Asus2  A     B  E  B  C#m    Asus2  A  B
Never, nev-er,      never, need.


|E        B  C#m |    Asus2  A      E |
|         B  C#m |    Asus2  A      E |  *Fade out*
```

Brass in Pocket

Words and Music by
Chrissie Hynde and James Honeyman-Scott

Melody:

I got brass _ in pock-et.

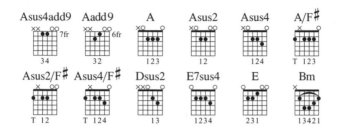

Asus4add9 Aadd9 A Asus2 Asus4 A/F#
Asus2/F# Asus4/F# Dsus2 E7sus4 E Bm

Intro
| Asus4add9 Aadd9 |

Verse 1

A Asus2 Asus4 A
I got brass   in pocket.

A Asus2 Asus4 A
Got bottle, I'm gonna use it.

A/F# Asus2/F# Asus4/F# A/F#
Intention,   I feel inventive.

Dsus2   E7sus4
Gonna make you, make you, make you notice.

Verse 2

A Asus2 Asus4 A
Got motion, restrained emotion.

A Asus2 Asus4 A
Been drivin', Detroit leanin'.

A/F# Asus2/F# Asus4/F# A/F#
No reason,   just seems so pleasin'.

Dsus2   E7sus4
Gonna make you, make you, make you notice.

Pre-Chorus 1

        E
    Gonna use my arms. Gonna use my legs.

    Gonna use my style. Gonna use my sidestep.

    Gonna use my fingers.

    Gonna use my, my, my 'magi-nation, oh.

Chorus 1

        A
    'Cause I gonna make you see

          Bm
    There's nobody else here,

    No one like me.

    Dsus2
    I'm special, so special,

    I gotta have some of your attention. Give it to me.

Verse 3

    A Asus2   **Asus4 A**
        I got rhythm,   I can't miss a beat.

    A Asus2   **Asus4 A**
        I got new skank,   so reet.

    A/F♯ Asus2/F♯   **Asus4/F♯ A/F♯**
        Got something;   I'm winkin' at you.

    Dsus2   **E7sus4**
        Gonna make you, make you, make you notice.

Pre-Chorus 2   *Repeat Pre-Chorus 1*

Chorus 2   *Repeat Chorus 1*

Chorus 3   *Repeat Chorus 1*

Outro

    | **A**   **Asus2** | **Asus4**   **A** |

    | **A**   **Asus2** | **Asus4**   **A** |
    Oh.   And when you

    | **A**   **Asus2** | **Asus4**   **A** |
    Walk.

    | **A**   **Asus2** | **Asus4add9 Aadd9** |

California Girls

Words and Music by
Brian Wilson and Mike Love

Melody:

Well, East Coast girls are hip, ___ I

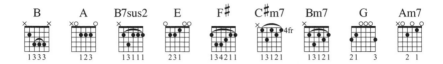

B   A   B7sus2   E   F♯   C♯m7   Bm7   G   Am7

Intro

||: B | :|| *Play 4 times*

| A | | B | | |

Verse 1

B
Well, East Coast girls are hip,

B7sus2
I really dig ___ those styles they wear.

E
And the Southern girls with the way they talk,

F♯
They knock me out when I'm down there.

B
The Midwest farmer's daughters

B7sus2
Really make you feel alright.

E
And the Northern girls with the way they kiss,

F♯
They keep their boyfriends warm at night.

Chorus 1

         B   **C#m7**
I wish they all could be ___ California

      A   **Bm7**
girls.
    (I wish they all could be ___ California...)

     G   **Am7**   **B**
I wish they all could be ___ California girls.

Verse 2

     B
The West Coast has the sunshine,

      B7sus2
And the girls all get so tan.

      E
I dig a French bikini on Hawaiian island dolls

     F#
By a palm tree in the sand.

    B
I've been all around this great big world

     B7sus2
And I've seen all kinds of girls.

      E
Yeah, but I couldn't wait to get back in the States,

      F#
Back to the cutest girls in the world.

Chorus 2   *Repeat Chorus 1*

Interlude | **B** | **C#m7** |

Outro

    B
‖: I wish they all could be California

  C#m7
girls.
    I wish they all could be California girls. :‖ *Repeat and fade*

Call Me the Breeze

Words and Music
by John Cale

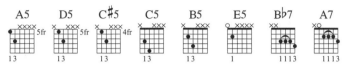

Intro ‖: A5 | | | :‖ *Play 4 times*

Verse 1
A5
Call me the breeze; I keep blowin' down the road.

D5
Well, now, they call me the breeze;

C#5   C5   B5   A5
I keep blowin' ___ down ___ the road.

E5
I ain't got me nobody;

D5   A5
   I don't carry me no load.

Verse 2
A5
Ain't no change in the weather,

Ain't no changes for me.

D5
Well, there ain't no change in the weather,

C#5 C5 B5   A5
Ain't no chang - es for me.

E5
And I ain't hidin' from nobody;

D5   A5
   Nobody's hidin' from me.

Oh, that's the way it's s'posed to be.

Guitar Solo	‖: A5				:‖	
	D5				C#5 C5 B5	
	A5					
	E5		D5			
	‖: A5				:‖	*Play 3 times*
	D5				C#5 C5 B5	
	A5					
	E5		D5			
	A5					

Verse 3

        A5
Well, I got that green light, baby;

I got to keep movin' on.

        D5
Well, I got that green light, babe;

      C#5   **C5** **B5** **A5**
I got to keep ___ mov - in' on.

        E5
Well, I might go out to California,

D5   **A5**
  Might go down to Georgia, I don't know.

Piano Solo	‖: A5			:‖	*Play 8 times*
	D5			C#5 C5 B5	
	A5				
	E5		D5	A5	

	A5
Verse 4	Well, I dig you Georgia peaches;

Makes me feel right at home.

      D5
Well, now, I dig you Georgia peaches;

        C#5 C5 B5   A5
Makes me feel ____ right at home.

      E5
But I don't love me no one woman,

D5   **A5**
  So I can't stay at Georgia's long.

         A5
Verse 5   Well, now, they call me the breeze;

I keep blowin' down the road.

      D5
Well, now, they call me the breeze;

    C#5   **C5**   **A5**
I keep blow-in' down ____ the road.

    E5
I ain't got me nobody,

D5   **A5 C#5 D5 D#5**
  I don't carry me no load.

E5 N.C.   **Bb7 A7**
Woo.   *Mister Breeze.*

Don't Do Me Like That

Words and Music
by Tom Petty

Melody:

I was talk-in' with a friend of mine, _

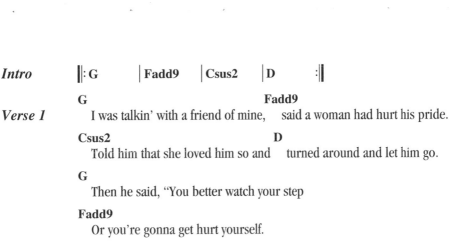

G	Fadd9	Csus2	D	Em7	C	G5	C5	Cm

Intro   ‖: G   │ Fadd9   │ Csus2   │ D   :‖

Verse 1

   G   Fadd9
I was talkin' with a friend of mine,   said a woman had hurt his pride.

   Csus2   D
Told him that she loved him so and   turned around and let him go.

   G
Then he said, "You better watch your step

   Fadd9
Or you're gonna get hurt yourself.

   Csus2   D
Someone's gonna tell you lies,   cut you down to size."

Chorus 1

   G   Fadd9
Don't do me like that,   don't do me like that.

   Em7   C   D
What if I loved you, baby?   Don't do me like that.

   G   Fadd9
Don't do me like that,   don't do me like that.

   Em7   C   D
Someday I might need you, baby.   Don't do me like that.

Verse 2

G   **Fadd9**
Listen, honey, can you see?   Baby, you would bury me

Csus2   **D**
If you were in a public eye   givin' someone else a try.

G
And you know you better watch your step

Fadd9
Or you're gonna get hurt yourself.

Csus2   **D**
Someone's gonna tell you lies,   cut you down to size.

Chorus 2

G   **Fadd9**
Don't do me like that,   don't do me like that.

Em7   **C**   **D**
What if I loved you, baby?   Don't, don't, don't, don't.

G   **Fadd9**
Don't do me like that,   don't do me like that.

Em7   **C**   **D**
What if I need you, baby?   Don't do me like that.

Bridge

         G5   **C5**
'Cause somewhere deep down inside someone is sayin',

         G5   **C5**
"Love ___ doesn't last that long."

G5   **C5**
I've had this feelin' inside night out and day in,

        Cm   **D**
And babe, I can't take it no more.

Verse 3   *Repeat Verse 2*

G   Fadd9
Chorus 3   Don't do me like that,   don't do me like that.

Em7   C   D
What if I loved you, baby?   Don't, don't, don't, don't.

G   Fadd9
Don't do me like that,   don't do me like that.

Em7   C   D
I just might need you, honey.   Don't do me like that. Now, wait.

G   Fadd9
Outro   Don't do me like that,   don't do me like that.

Em7   C   D
Baby, baby, baby.   Don't, don't, don't, don't.

G   Fadd9
Don't do me like that,   don't do me like that.

Em7   C   D
Baby, baby, baby.   Oh, oh, oh.

| G | Fadd9 | Em7 | C   D | *Fade out*

Cat Scratch Fever

Words and Music
by Ted Nugent

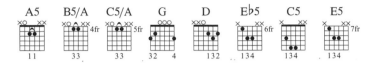

A5   B5/A   C5/A   G   D   Eb5   C5   E5

Intro

‖: A5 B5/A C5/A | A5 B5/A C5/A |
| A5 B5/A C5/A | B5/A A5 :‖ *Play 4 times*

Verse 1

N.C.   A5   C5/A   A5
Well, I don't know where they come from,

C5/A   A5 C5/A   A5   N.C.
But they sure do   come.

G   D   A5 C5/A A5
  I hope they comin' for me.

C5/A A5   C5/A   A5
And I don't know how they do it,

C5/A   A5 C5/A   A5   N.C.
But they sure do it   good.

G   D   A5 C5/A A5
  I hope they doin' it for free.

Chorus 1

N.C.   A5 B5/A C5/A   A5 B5/A C5/A
They give me cat scratch fever,

A5 B5/A   C5/A   B5/A A5
Cat scratch fever.

Verse 2

N.C.   A5   C5/A A5
Well, the first time that I got it

C5/A A5 C5/A   A5 N.C.
I was   just ten years old.

 G   D   A5   C5/A A5
I got it from some kitty next door.

C5/A N.C.   A5   C5/A A5
I   went to see the doctor

C5/A A5 C5/A A5   N.C.
And he gave me the cure.

G   D   A5   C5/A A5
  I think I got it some more.

Chorus 2

N.C.   A5 B5/A C5/A A5 B5/A C5/A N.C.
They give me cat scratch fever,

A5 B5/A C5/A B5/A A5
Cat scratch fever.

N.C. A5 B5/A C5/A A5 B5/A C5/A N.C.
I got a bad scratch fever,

   A5 B5/A C5/A B5/A A5
The cat scratch fever.

Bridge

Eb5   C5   Eb5
   It's nothin' dang'rous,   I feel no pain.

             C5
I got to try, try, try.

Eb5
   You know you got it when

C5   Eb5
   You're goin' insane.

              E5
It makes a grown man cry, cry.

              N.C.
Oh, won't you bite my fur.

Guitar Solo

```
| A5  B5/A  C5/A     | A5  B5/A  C5/A  N.C.|
| A5  B5/A  C5/A     |     B5/A  A5    N.C. |
| A5  B5/A  C5/A     | A5  B5/A  C5/A  N.C.|
| A5  B5/A  C5/A     |     B5/A  A5        D5|
|         E5      C5 |         D5    N.C.  |
| A5  B5/A  C5/A     | A5  B5/A  C5/A  N.C.|
| A5  B5/A  C5/A     |     B5/A  A5         |
```

Verse 3

N.C.   A5   C5/A A5
Well, I make a pussy purr

C5/A A5   C5/A A5 N.C.
With a stroke of my hand.

G   D   A5   C5/A   A5
  They know they gettin' it from me.

C5/A N.C.   A5   C5/A   A5
And   they   know just where to go

C5/A   A5   C5/A   A5   N.C.
When they need their lovin' ___ man.

G   D   A5 C5/A   A5
  They know I'm doin' it for free.

Chorus 3

N.C.   A5 B5/A C5/A A5 B5/A C5/A N.C.
I give 'em cat scratch fever,

A5 B5/A C5/A B5/A A5
Cat scratch fever.

N.C.   A5 B5/A C5/A A5 B5/A C5/A N.C.
They got it bad scratch fever,

A5 B5/A C5/A B5/A A5   N.C.
A cat scratch fever.   Hey!

Breakdown

A5 B5/A C5/A	A5 B5/A C5/A	
A5 B5/A C5/A	B5/A A5 N.C. A5
B5/A C5/A	A5 B5/A C5/A	
A5 B5/A C5/A	B5/A A5 N.C.	

Chorus 4

A5 B5/A C5/A A5 B5/A C5/A N.C.
‖: Cat scratch fever,

A5 B5/A C5/A   B5/A A5 N.C.
Cat scratch fever.   :‖ *Play 3 times*

Outro

A5 B5/A C5/A			
A5	B5/A	A5	
Yeah,	yeah, yeah, yeah, yeah, yeah!		

                  Yeow!

Caught Up in You

Words and Music by Frank Sullivan,
Jim Peterik, Jeff Carlisi and Don Barnes

Melody:

I nev - er __ knew __ there'd come __

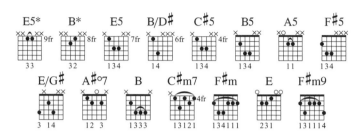

| E5* | B* | E5 | B/D# | C#5 | B5 | A5 | F#5 |

| E/G# | A#°7 | B | C#m7 | F#m | E | F#m9 |

Intro

‖: **E5*   B*   │E5*   B*   :‖**

Verse 1

E5 B/D# C#5   B5   A5   C#5 B5
I never   knew there'd come a day

When I'd be sayin' to you,

E5   B/D# C#5   B5 A5   C#5 B5
"Don't let this good love slip a-way,

              A5
Now that we know that it's true."

     C#5   B5   A5
Don't,   don't you know the kind of man I am?

     C#5   B5   A5 F#5
No,   said I'd never fall in love a-gain.

      E/G#   A5   A#°7   B5
But it's real and the feeling comes shining through.

Chorus 1

                                                    A5   E/G#
I'm so caught up in you, ___ little girl,

        F#5   C#5
And I never did suspect a thing.

        E5   A5   E/G#
So caught up in you, little girl,

        F#5   C#5
That I never wanna get myself free.

        E5   A5
And baby, it's true.

            E/G#   F#5
You're the one who caught me,

E/G#   A5   A#°7   B
Baby, you taught me how good it could be.

            E5   B/D# C#5   B5   A5   C#5   B5
Verse 2   It took so long to change my mind.

I thought that love was a game.

E5   B/D#   C#5   B5   A5   C#5   B5
   I played a-round e-nough to find

                        A5
No two are ever the same.

        C#5   B5   A5
You   made me realize the love I'd missed.

        C#5 B5   A5 F#5
So   hot, love I couldn't quite re-sist.

            E/G#   A5   A#°7   B5
When it's right the light just comes shining through.

Chorus 2

                        A5   **E/G#**
I'm so caught up in you, ___ little girl,

         F#5   **C#5**
You're the one that's got me down on my knees.

   E5   **A5**   **E/G#**
So caught up in you, little girl,

     F#5   **C#5**
That I never wanna get myself free.

     E5   **A5**
And baby, it's true.

       E/G#   **F#5**
You're the one who caught me,

E/G#   **A5**   **A#°7**   **B**
Baby, you taught me how good it could be.

          C#m7   **F#m**
Bridge   Fill your days ___ and your nights,

         B   **E**   **C#m7**
No need to ever ask me twice, ___ oh, no,

F#m9   **B**
  Whenever you want __me.

     C#m7   **F#m**
And if ev - er comes a day

          B   **E5**
When you should turn and walk away,

B/D# **C#m7** **F#m**   **B5**
Oh,   no,   I can't live without ___ you.

I'm so caught up in you.

Guitar Solo | A5   E/G# | F#5 | C#5 | E5 A5 |

                   | E/G# | F#5 | C#5 | E5 A5 |

                   | E/G# | F#5 | E/G#A5 | A#°7 B5 |

                    B5 C#m7   F#m
Interlude   And if ev - er comes a day

                              B   E5
              When you should turn and walk away,

              B/D# C#m7 F#m   B5
              Oh,   no.   I can't live without ____ you.

                              A5   E/G#
Chorus 3   I'm so caught up in you, little girl,

                      F#5   C#5
              You're the one that's got me down on my knees.

                  E5   A5   E/G#
              So caught up in you, little girl,

                      F#5   C#5
              That I never wanna get myself free.

              E5   A5
              And baby, it's true.

                      E/G#   F#5   E/G#
              You're the one who caught me, baby,

                  A5   B5   A5
              You taught me how good it could be.

                  E/G#   F#5   C#5
              Little girl, you're the one that's got me down on my knees.

                  E5   A5   E/G#
              So caught up in you little girl

                      F#5   C#5
              That I never wanna get myself free.

              E5   A5   E/G#
              And baby, it's true. You're the one

                      F#5   E/G#
              Who caught me, an' taught me,

              A5   B5   A5
              An' got me so caught up in you.

Outro   ‖:A5   E/G#| F#5| C#5 | E5 A5 |
              | E/G#| F#5| C#5 | E5 A5 |
              | E/G#| F#5| E/G# A5 | B5 A5:‖ *Repeat and fade*

CLASSIC ROCK   57

Changes

Words and Music
by David Bowie

Melody:

I still don't know what I ____ was

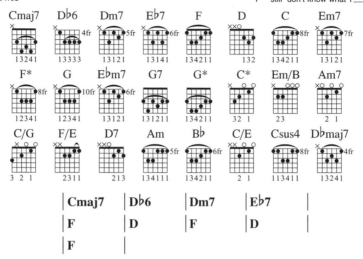

Cmaj7   Db6   Dm7   Eb7   F   D   C   Em7
F*   G   Ebm7   G7   G*   C*   Em/B   Am7
C/G   F/E   D7   Am   Bb   C/E   Csus4   Dbmaj7

Intro

Cmaj7	Db6	Dm7	Eb7	
F	D	F	D	
F	

Verse 1

      C   Em7
I still don't know what I was   waiting for

         F*   G
And my time was running wild.

            F*
A million dead ____end streets,

          C   Em7
And ____ ev'ry time I thought I'd   got it made

         F*   G
It seemed the taste was not so sweet.

        Cmaj7   Dm7   Em7   Ebm7
So I turned my-self to face ____ me

        Dm7   G7
But I've never caught a glimpse

        Cmaj7   Dm7   Em7
How the others must see the fak-er,

Ebm7   Dm7
  I'm much too fast to take that test.

Chorus 1

G*   F
(Ch, ch, ch, ch, changes.)

C*   Em/B   Am7
Turn and face the strange.

                  C/G
(Ch, ch, chang - es.)

F   F/E   D7
Don't want to be a rich-er man.

G*   F
(Ch, ch, ch, ch, changes.)

C*   Em/B   Am7
Turn and face the strange.

                  C/G
(Ch, ch chang - es.)

F   F/E   D7
Just gonna have to be a dif-f'rent man.

Am G* B♭   F   C/E D7 G7 C*
Time may change me but I   can't trace time.

Interlude |D |F |D |F |

Verse 2

C   Em7
I watch the ripples   change their size

  F*   G
But never leave the stream

                F*   C
Of warm imper - manence and ___ so the days float

Em7   F*   G
Through my eyes but still ___ the days seem the same.

        Cmaj7 Dm7   Em7
And these children ___ that you ___ spit on

E♭m7   Dm7   G7
As they try to change their worlds

        Cmaj7   Dm7   Em7
Are im-mune to your consulta-tions.

E♭m7   Dm7
They're quite a-ware what they're going through.

Chorus 2

G*   F
(Ch, ch, ch, ch, changes.)

C*   Em/B   Am7
Turn and face the strange.

       C/G
(Ch, ch, chang - es.)

F   F/E   D7
Don't tell them to grow up and out of it.

G*   F
(Ch, ch, ch, ch, changes.)

C*   Em/B   Am7
Turn and face the strange.

       C/G
(Ch, ch chang - es.)

F   F/E   D7
Where's your shame? You've left us up to our necks in it.

Am G* B♭ F C/E D7 G7 C* Dm7 Em7
Time may change me but you can't trace time.

Bridge

F*   C   Csus4 C
Strange fascination fas-cinating me.

 F*   G   F
Oh, changes are taking the pace I'm going through.

Chorus 3

G*   F
(Ch, ch, ch, ch, changes.)

C*   Em/B   Am7 C/G
Turn and face the strange.

F   F/E   D7
 Oo, look out   you rock 'n' roll-ers.

G*   F
(Ch, ch, ch, ch, changes.)

C*   Em/B   Am7
Turn and face the strange.

           C/G
(Ch, ch, chang - es.)

F   F/E   D7
Pretty soon now ____ you're gonna get old-er.

Am G* B♭   F   C/E D7 G7 C*
Time may change me but I   can't trace time.

         Am G* B♭   F   C/E D7 G7 C* Dm7
I said that time may change me but I   can't trace time.
| Em7 | E♭7 | Dm7 | D♭maj7 | Cmaj7 |

Day Tripper

Words and Music by
John Lennon and Paul McCartney

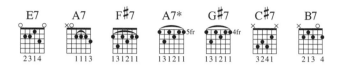

E7   A7   F#7   A7*   G#7   C#7   B7

Intro | E7 | ‖: E7 | | | :‖

E7

Verse 1   Got a good reason

For taking the easy way out.

A7
Got a good reason

   E7
For taking the easy way out, now.

     F#7
She was a day tripper,

One way ticket, yeah.

     A7* G#7   **C#7**
It took me so   long to find out,

     B7
And I found out.

| E7 | | | |

Verse 2

E7
She's a big teaser,

She took me half the way there.
A7
She's a big teaser,
E7
She took me half the way there, now.
      F#7
She was a day tripper,

One way ticket, yeah.
     A7*G#7   C#7
It took me so   long to find out,
       B7
And I found out.

Solo

‖: B7 | | | :‖ *Play 3 times*

| E7 | | | |

Verse 3

E7
Tried to please her,

She only played one night stands.
A7
Tried to please her,
E7
She only played one night stands, now.
     F#7
She was a day tripper,

Sunday driver, yeah.
     A7*G#7   C#7
It took me so   long to find out,
       B7
And I found out.

Outro

‖: E7 | | | :‖

‖: Day tripper, day tripper, yeah.

Day tripper, day tripper, yeah. :‖ *Repeat and fade*

Do You Feel Like We Do

Words and Music by Peter Frampton,
John Siomos, Rick Wills and Mick Gallagher

Melody:

Woke up this morn-ing with a

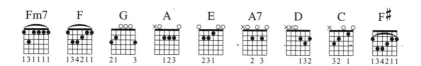

Fm7	F	G	A	E	A7	D	C	F#
131111	134211	21 3	123	231	2 3	132	32 1	134211

Intro . |Fm7 | | |F G |

Verse 1

    A   **E**
Woke up this morning with a wine glass in my hand.

    A
Whose wine, what wine, where the hell did I dine?

                                  E
Must have been a dream, I don't be-lieve where I've been.

    A   **A7**
Come on,   let's do it again.

Chorus 1

    D   **F** **C** **G**   **D**
Do you, you feel like I do?

            F **C** **G**   **D**
Do you, you feel like I do?

	A E
Verse 2	My friend got busted just the other day.

A
My friend got busted just the other day.

A
Don't walk, don't walk, don't walk away.

                                        E
Drove into a taxi, bent the boot, hit the back.

A   **A7**
Had to play some music,   otherwise he'd crack.

D   **F**   **C**   **G**   **D**
Chorus 2   Do you, you feel like I do?

              F   **C**   **G**
Do you, you feel like I...

A   **E**
Verse 3   Champagne for breakfast and a Sherman in my hand.

A
Peach top, peach tails, never fails.

                                        E
Must have been a dream, I don't be-lieve where I've been.

A   **A7**
Come on,   let's do it again.

Chorus 3   *Repeat Chorus 2*

Outro | N.C. | | **F♯** | **G** | **D**

Don't Fear the Reaper

Words and Music
by Donald Roeser

Melody:

All _____ our times _____ have __ come. __

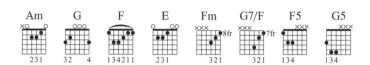

| Am | G | F | E | Fm | G7/F | F5 | G5 |

Intro ‖: Am   G |F   G   :‖ *Play 4 times*

Verse 1

Am G   F   G   Am   G   F   G
All ___ our times __ have __ come.

Am G   F   G   Am   G   F   G
Here ____ but now __ they're __ gone.

Chorus 1

F   G   Am
Seasons don't fear the reap - er,

            F   E   Am
Nor do the wind, the sun or the rain.

        G   F
We can be like they ___ are.

G   Am   G   F   G   Am
Come on, ba - by, don't fear the reap - er. Baby, take my hand.

        G   F   G   Am
Don't fear the reap - er. We'll be able to fly.

        G   F   G   Am   G   F   G
Don't fear the reap - er. Baby, I'm your man.

Am G   F   G Am   G   F   G
La, ____ la, la, __ la, __ la.

Am G   F   G Am   G   F   G
La, ____ la, la, __ la, __ la.

|Am   G |F   G |Am | |

Interlude 1   *Repeat Intro*

Verse 2

Am G   **F**   **G**   **Am**   **G**   **F**   **G**
Val - entine __ is __ done.

Am **G**   **F**   **G**   **Am** **G**   **F**   **G**
Here ____ but now __ they're __ gone.

Chorus 2

F   **G**   **Am**   **F**   **E** **Am** **G**
   Rome-o and Ju - liet are to-gether in e-ternity.

F   **G**   **Am**   **G**
Forty thousand men and woman ev - 'ry day.

F   **G**   **Am**   **G**
Forty thousand men and woman ev - 'ry day.

  F   **G**   **Am**   **G**   **F**
An-other forty thousand coming ev - 'ry day.

G   **Am**   **G**   **F**
Come on, ba - by. (Don't fear the reap - er.)

     G   **Am**   **G**   **F**
Baby, take my hand.   (Don't fear the reap - er.)

       G   **Am**   **G**   **F**
We'll be able to fly.   (Don't fear the reap - er.)

      G   **Am**   **G**   **F**   **G**
Baby, I'm your man.

Am G   **F**   **G Am**   **G**   **F**   **G**
La, ____ la, la, __ la, __ la.

Am G   **F**   **G Am**   **G**   **F**   **G**
La, ____ la, la, __ la, __ la.

| **Am** **G** | **F** **G** | **Am** | | |

Interlude 2   ‖: **Fm** | | **G7/F** | :‖

Guitar Solo   ‖: **Fm** | | **G7/F** | :‖ *Play 4 times*
            | **F5** | | **G5** | |
            | **F5** | | **G5** | |

Interlude 3   *Repeat Intro*

Verse 3

| Am | G | | F | G | Am | | G | F | G |
Love __ of two __ is __ one.

| Am | G | | F | | G | Am | G | F | | G |
Here __ but now __ they're __ gone.

Chorus 3

| F | | G | | Am |
Came the last night of sad - ness,

| | F | G | | Am | G |
And it was clear she couldn't go on.

| | F | | G | | | Am | | G |
And the door was o - pen and the wind ___ appeared.

| | F | | G | | Am | G |
The candles blew __ and then dis-appeared.

| | F | | G | | Am |
The curtains flew __ and then he appeared.

| | G | | F | G | | Am |
Said don't be afraid. __ Come on, ba - by.

| | G | | F | G | | Am |
And she had no fear. __   And she ran ___ to him.

| | G | | F | | G |
(Then they started to fly.) __ They looked backward

| | Am |
And said ___ goodbye.

| | G | | F | | | G | | Am |
(She had be-come like they __ are.) She had taken his hand.

| | G | | F |
(She had be-come like they __ are.)

| G | | Am | | G | | F | G |
Come on, ba - by. (Don't fear the reap - er.)

Outro   ‖: Am   G | F   G   :‖ *Repeat and fade*

Every Little Thing She Does Is Magic

Music and Lyrics
by Sting

Melody:

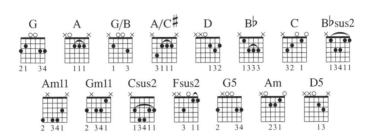

Though I've   tried be - fore _ to   tell _ her

| G | A | G/B | A/C# | D | Bb | C | Bbsus2 |

| Am11 | Gm11 | Csus2 | Fsus2 | G5 | Am | D5 |

Intro   ‖: G   A | G/B   A/C# :‖

                                  G   A

Verse 1   Though I've tried before to tell ___ her

                      G/B   A/C#   G   A   G/B   A/C#
Of the feel - ings I have for her in my ___ heart,

                  G   A   G/B
Ev'ry time ___ that I come near ___ her I just lose ___ my nerve

           A/C#   D
As I've ___ done from the start.

                  A   D

Chorus 1   Ev-'ry little thing she does is mag - ic,

                        A   D
Ev'rything she does just turns me on.

                        A   D
Even though my life before was trag - ic,

                        A   Bb   C   G   A   G/B A/C#
Now I know my love for her goes on.

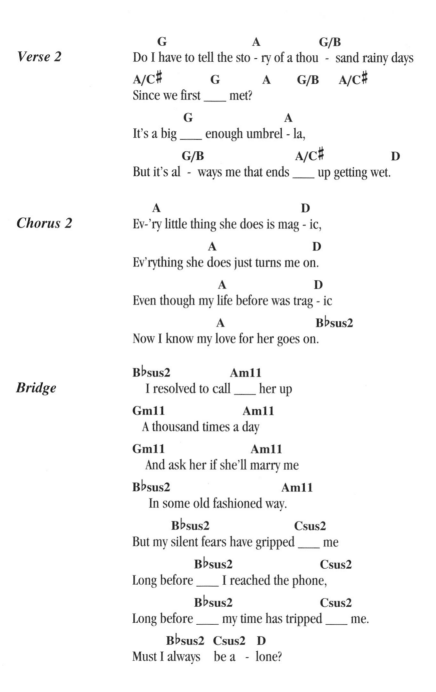

Verse 2

G   A   G/B
Do I have to tell the sto - ry of a thou - sand rainy days

A/C♯   G A G/B A/C♯
Since we first ____ met?

     G   A
It's a big ____ enough umbrel - la,

    G/B   A/C♯   D
But it's al - ways me that ends ____ up getting wet.

Chorus 2

    A   D
Ev-'ry little thing she does is mag - ic,

       A   D
Ev'rything she does just turns me on.

       A   D
Even though my life before was trag - ic

       A   B♭sus2
Now I know my love for her goes on.

Bridge

B♭sus2   Am11
 I resolved to call ____ her up

Gm11   Am11
 A thousand times a day

Gm11   Am11
 And ask her if she'll marry me

B♭sus2   Am11
 In some old fashioned way.

    B♭sus2   Csus2
But my silent fears have gripped ____ me

     B♭sus2   Csus2
Long before ____ I reached the phone,

     B♭sus2   Csus2
Long before ____ my time has tripped ____ me.

    B♭sus2 Csus2 D
Must I always be a - lone?

Chorus 3

           A   **D**
Ev-'ry little thing she does is mag - ic,

                A   **D**
Ev'rything she do just turns me on.

                  A   **D**
Even though my life before was trag - ic,

                A   **D**
Now I know my love for her goes on.

           A   **D**
Ev-'ry little thing she does is mag - ic,

                A   **D**
Ev'rything she do just turns me on.

                A   **D**
Even though my life before was trag - ic

           A
Now I know my love for her goes on.

Outro

‖: B♭ Fsus2 | G5 Am | B♭ Fsus2 | D5   :‖ *Repeat and fade*

Drive My Car

Words and Music by
John Lennon and Paul McCartney

Melody:

Asked a girl what she want-ed to be,

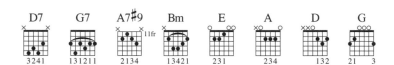

| D7 | G7 | A7#9 | Bm | E | A | D | G |

Intro
| D7 | | |

Verse 1

D7　　　　　　　　**G7**
　Asked a girl what she wanted to be,

D7　　　　　**G7**
　She said, baby, can't you see?

D7　　　　　　　　　**G7**
　I wanna be famous, a star of the screen,

　A7#9
But you can do something in between.

Chorus 1

Bm　　　　　　　　　**G7 Bm**　　　　　　**G7**
Baby, you can drive my car, yes I'm gonna be a star,

Bm　　　　　　　　**E**　　　**A**　　　**D**　　　**G A**
Baby, you can drive my car, and maybe I'll love you.

Verse 2

D7　　　　　　　　　**G7**
　I told that girl that my prospects were good,

D7　　　　　　　**G7**
　She said, baby, it's understood.

D7　　　　　　　　**G7**
　Working for peanuts is all very fine,

　A7#9
But I can show you a better time.

Chorus 2

Bm   G7 Bm   G7
Baby, you can drive my car, yes I'm gonna be a star,

Bm   E   A   D   G
Baby, you can drive my car, and maybe I'll love you.

A N.C.
Beep, beep, mm, beep, beep, yeah!

Solo

| D7 | G7 | D7 | G7 | |
| D7 | G7 | A | | |

Chorus 3

Repeat Chorus 1

Verse 3

D7   G7
I told that girl I could start right away,

D7   G7
And she said, listen, babe, I've got something to say,

D7   G7
I've got no car, and it's breaking my heart,

A7#9
But I've found a driver, and that's a start.

Chorus 4

Bm   G7 Bm   G7
Baby, you can drive my car, yes I'm gonna be a star,

Bm   E   A   D   G
Baby, you can drive my car, and maybe I'll love you.

A N.C.   D   G
Beep, beep, mm, beep, beep, yeah!

    A   D   G
‖: Beep, beep, mm, beep, beep, yeah!   :‖ *Repeat and fade*

Eight Miles High

Words and Music by Roger McGuinn,
David Crosby and Gene Clark

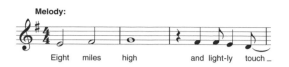

Melody:

Eight   miles   high   and light-ly   touch _

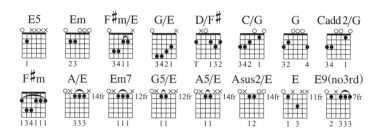

| E5 | Em | F#m/E | G/E | D/F# | C/G | G | Cadd2/G |
| F#m | A/E | Em7 | G5/E | A5/E | Asus2/E | E | E9(no3rd) |

Intro   ‖: N.C.(E5) | | :‖ **Play 4 times**

Verse 1
Em F#m/E G/E D/F#   C/G
Eight miles   high   and lightly touch ____ down,

G   D/F#   C/G Cadd2/G C/G Cadd2/G
You'll find that it's stranger than   known.

Em F#m/E G/E   D/F#   C/G
Signs in the _____ street   that say where you're ____ going,

G   D/F#   C/G Cadd2/G C/G Cadd2/G
Out some-where just being a - lone.

| Em   F#m/E | G/E   F#m/E |

Verse 2
Em F#m/E G/E D/F#   C/G
No - where   is   there warmth to be ____ found

G   D/F#   C/G Cadd2/G C/G Cadd2/G
Among those afraid of los-ing their ground.

Em F#m/E   G/E D/F#   C/G
Rain-grey   town   known for it's ____ sound,

G   D/F#   C/G Cadd2/G C/G Cadd2/G
In places ____ small faces un - bound.

Guitar Solo

```
| Em    F#m | Em    F#m | Em              |
| A/E       | Em7  A/E  |           Em7   |
|        A/E|           | Em7             |
| A/E       | Em7       | A/E             |
| Em7   A/E |           | Em7             |
| A/E       | Em7       | A/E             |
| G5/E A5/E |           | Em7             |
| A5/E Em7  |           | Asus2/E         |
|           |           |                 |
```

Verse 3

Em   F#m/E G/E   D/F#   C/G
'Round the   squares   huddled in ___ storms,

G   D/F#
  Some laughing, ___ some just

        C/G   Cadd2/G C/G Cadd2/G
Shape-less ___ forms.

Em   F#m/E G/E   D/F#   C/G
Side - walk   scenes   and black limo - sines,

G   D/F#   C/G   Cadd2/G   C Cadd2/G
  Some living, ___ some standing a   -   lone.

Outro

```
| Em    F#m | Em    F#m | Em              |
| A5/E      | G5/E A5/E |                 |
| G5/E      | A5/E      | Em7             |
| Asus2/E   | Em7       | Asus2/E         |
| Em7       | Asus2/E   | G5/E            |
| Asus2/E   | G5/E      | E               |
|    E9(no3rd)|         |                 |
```

Evil Woman

Words and Music
by Jeff Lynne

Melody:

You made a   fool of me, _____

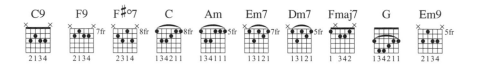

C9   F9   F#°7   C   Am   Em7   Dm7   Fmaj7   G   Em9

Intro

> **C9**
> You made a fool of me,
>
> **F9**   **F#°7**   **C**
> But them broken dreams ___ have got to end.
>
> ‖: **Am   Em7   Dm7** | **Em7** :‖ *Play 3 times*
> | **Am   Em7   Dm7** | **Em7   Am** |

Verse 1

>   **Em7   Dm7**
> Hey, wom - an, you got the blues.
>
> **Em7   Am**   **Em7   Dm7**
> Guess you ___ ain't got no ___ one else to use.
>
> **Em7   Am**   **Em7   Dm7**
> There's an open road ___ that leads nowhere,
>
> **Em7   Am**   **Em7   Dm7**
> So just ___ make some miles ___ between here and there.
>
> **Em7   Am**   **Em7   Dm7   Em7**
> There's a hole in my head ___ where the rain comes in.
>
> **Am**   **Em7   Dm7**   **Em7   Am**
> You took my body and played to win.
>
>   **Em7   Dm7**
> Ha, ha, woman it's a cryin' shame.
>
> **Em7   Fmaj7   G**   **C**
> But you ain't got no - body else ___ to blame.

Chorus 1

Am Em7 Dm7   Em7 Am Em7   Dm7   Em7 Am
E - vil   woman,   e - vil   woman.

  Em7 Dm7   Em7 Am Em7 Dm7   Em7 Am
E - vil woman,   e - vil woman.

Verse 2

Am   Em7   Dm7
  Rolled in ____ from anoth - er town.

Em7   Am   Em7 Dm7   Em7
Hit some ____ gold too hot to settle down.

  Am   Em7   Dm7   Em7
But a fool and his mon - ey soon go sep'rate ways.

Am   Em7   Dm7   Em7 Am
  You found a fool lyin' ____ in a daze.

      Em7   Dm7
Ha, ha, woman what you gonna do?

Em7 Am   Em7   Dm7   Em7 Am
You de-stroyed all the vir-tues that the Lord gave you.

       Em7   Dm7
It's so good ____ that you're feelin' pain,

Em7 Fmaj7   G   C
But you better get your face on board the very next train. (Train.)

Chorus 2

Am Em7 Dm7   Em7 Am Em7 Dm7   Em7 Am
  E - vil   woman,   e - vil woman.

  Em7 Dm7   Em7   Am
E - vil   woman, (You're an evil ____ wom-an.)

  Em7 Dm7 Em7 Am
E - vil woman.

String Solo

	Em7 Dm7		Em7	Am	Em7 Dm7
	Em7 Am		Em7 Am		Em7 Dm7
	Em7	Am Em7 Dm7		Em7 Am	
(Hey, hey, hey, hey!)
| | Em7 Dm7 | Em7 | | Am Em7 Dm7 |
| | Em7 Am | Em7 Dm7 | | Em7 |
(Hey, hey, hey, hey!)
| Fmaj7 G | Dm7 | Em9 | |
(Hey, hey, hey.)

Chorus 3	*Repeat Chorus 2*
	Em7 **Dm7** **Em7 Am**
Verse 3	Evil woman, how you done me wrong,

               Em7   **Dm7**   **Em7 Am**
But now you try ___ to wail a dif'rent song.

           Em7   **Dm7**   **Em7 Am**
Ha, ha, funny how you broke me up.

                 Em7   **Dm7**   **Em7 Am**
You made the wine, ___ now you drink the cup.

            Em7   **Dm7**   **Em7 Am**
I came a runnin' ev -'ry time you cried.

            Em7   **Dm7**   **Em7 Am**
Thought I ___ saw love smilin' in your eyes.

            Em7 **Dm7**
Ha, ha, ___ ver-y nice to know

Em7   **Fmaj7**   **G**   **C**
That you   ain't got no ___ place a left to go. (Go.)

Chorus 4	*Repeat Chorus 1*
	Am Em7 Dm7 **Em7 Am Em7 Dm7**
Outro	E - vil woman, e - vil woman.

            Em7 Am
(You're an evil   woman.)

        Em7 Dm7   **Em7**   **Am**   **Em7 Dm7**
E - vil   woman, (Such an evil ___ wom-an.) e - vil   woman.

             Em7 Am   **Em7 Dm7**
(You're an evil woman.) E - vil   woman.

             Em7   **Am Em7 Dm7**
(Such an evil ___ wom-an.)   ***Fade out***

For Your Love

Words and Music by Graham Gouldman

Melody:

(For your love.) —

| Em | G | A | Am | B5 | A5 | E5 | C# | B |

Intro

| Em | G | A | Am |

| Em | G | A | Am |
(For your love.)

| Em | G | A | Am |
(For your love.)

| Em | G | A | Am |
(For your love.)

Verse 1

Em   G
   I'd give you ev - 'rything

   A   Am
And more, and that's for sure.   (For your love.)

Em   G
   I'd bring you dia - mond rings

   A   Am
And things right to your door.   (For your love.)

Em   G
   To thrill you with __ delight,

A   Am
   I'd give you dia - monds bright.

Em   G
   There'll be days I will __ excite

A   Am
   To make you dream of me __ at night.

	Em G A Am
Chorus	(For your love.) _____

	Em G A Am
	(For your love.) _____

	Em G A Am Em N.C.
	(For your love.) _____

	B5
Bridge	For your love,

For your love,

    A5   E5
I would give the stars above.

    B5
For your love,

For your love,

    A5   C#   B
I would give you all I could. _____

Interlude   *Repeat Intro*

Verse 2

     Em   **G**
     I'd give the moon

  A   **Am**
If it were mine to give.   (For your love.)

     Em   **G**
     I'd give the stars

      A   **Am**
And the sun 'fore I'd live.   (For your love.)

     Em   **G**
     To thrill you with __ delight,

A   **Am**
     I'd give you dia - monds bright.

     Em   **G**
     There'll be days I will __ excite,

A   **Am**
     To make you dream of me __ at night.

Outro

          Em G A Am
(For your love.)

          Em G A Am
(For your love.)

          Em G A Am
(For your love.)

          Em G A Am Em
(For your love.)

Free Ride

Words and Music
by Dan Hartman

Melody:

The moun-tain is high, _____ the val-ley is low _

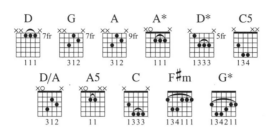

| D | G | A | A* | D* | C5 |
| D/A | A5 | C | F#m | G* | |

Intro   D ‖: G A   G D |G   D A*   D :‖ *Play 3 times*
          |G A   G D |G   D A* |

Verse 1
          D*   C5   A*   D/A A5
The moun-tain is high, the val-ley is low

          D*   C   A*   D/A   A5
And you're ___ con-fused on which way to go.

          D*   C   A*   D/A   A*
So I've ___ come here to give you a hand

          D*   C   A*   D/A   A*
And lead ___ you into the promised land.

Chorus 1
          F#m   G*   A5
So, (Ooh.) come on ___ and take a free ride.

             F#m   G*   D*
(Free ride. Ooh.) Come on ___ and stand here by my side.

       F#m   G*   D*
(Ooh.) Come on ___ and take a free ride.

Guitar Solo 1   ‖: G A   G D |G   D A*   D :‖ *Play 3 times*
          |G   A   G   D |G   D A* |

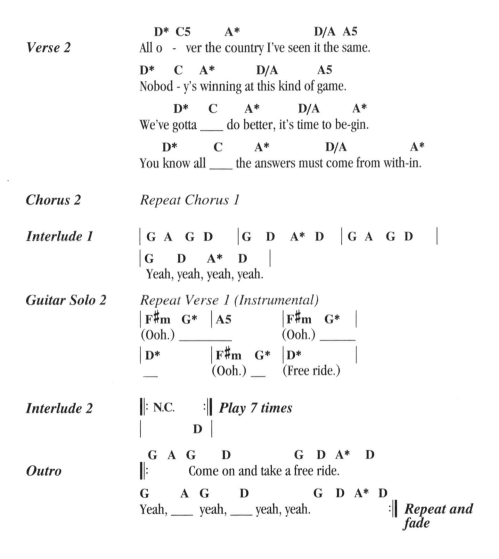

Verse 2

D* C5   A*   D/A A5
All o - ver the country I've seen it the same.

D*   C A*   D/A   A5
Nobod - y's winning at this kind of game.

     D*   C   A*   D/A   A*
We've gotta ___ do better, it's time to be-gin.

    D*   C   A*   D/A   A*
You know all ___ the answers must come from with-in.

Chorus 2   *Repeat Chorus 1*

Interlude 1 | G A G D |G D A* D |G A G D |

| G   D A* D |
Yeah, yeah, yeah, yeah.

Guitar Solo 2   *Repeat Verse 1 (Instrumental)*

| F#m G* |A5 |F#m G* |
(Ooh.) _____   (Ooh.) _____

| D* |F#m G* |D* |
___   (Ooh.) ___ (Free ride.)

Interlude 2 ||: N.C.   :|| *Play 7 times*

| D |

Outro

   G A G   D   G D A* D
||:   Come on and take a free ride.

G   A G   D   G D A* D
Yeah, ___ yeah, ___ yeah, yeah.   :|| *Repeat and fade*

Gloria

Words and Music
by Van Morrison

Melody:

Like to tell you 'bout __ my   ba - by.

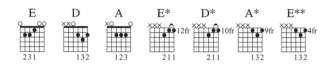

E   D   A   E*   D*   A*   E**

Intro   ‖: E   D   A │ E   D   A   :‖

			E D A

Verse 1   Like to tell you 'bout my baby.

E   D   A   E   D A
You know she comes around.

E   D A   E   D   A
Just 'bout five feet four,

E   D   A   E   D   A
A from her head to the __ ground.

E   D   A   E   D A
You know she comes around ___ here,

E   D A   E   D   A
A just a-bout midnight.

E   D   A   E   D   A
She make me feel so good, Lord.

E   D   A E   D   A
She make me feel al - right.

E   D   A
And her name is

E D A E   D A E   D A E   D A E
G   L,   O,   R,   I.

D A E   D A E
G, L, O, R, I, A.

<pre>
                E   D   A   E   D A E
Chorus 1   (Glo - ri - a.) G, L, O, R, I, A.
                      D   A   E   D   A E
           (Glo   - ri - a.) I'm gonna shout it all __ night.
                      D   A   E   D   A E
           (Glo   - ri - a.) I'm gonna shout it ev-'ry day.
                      D   A   E   D   A   E
           (Glo   - ri - a.) Yeah, yeah, yeah, yeah, yeah, yeah, yeah.
           | E   D   A | E   D   A |
</pre>

<pre>
Interlude ‖: E*   D*   A*   D* | E*   D*   A*   D* :‖   Play 3 times
           ‖: E**   D   A | E**   D   A   :‖
           | E | |
</pre>

<pre>
                             E
Verse 2   She comes around here, just about midnight.

           Ha, she make me feel so good, Lord. I wanna say she make me feel alright.

           Comes walkin' down my street. Watch her come up to my house.

           You knock upon my door. And then she comes to my room.

           Then she make me feel alright.

           G, L, O, R, I, A.
</pre>

<pre>
                E   D   A   E   D A E
Chorus 2   (Glo - ri - a.) G, L, O, R, I, A.
                      D   A   E   D   A E
           (Glo   - ri - a.) I'm gonna shout it all __ night.
                      D   A   E   D   A E
           (Glo   - ri - a.) I'm gonna shout it ev-'ry day.
                      D   A   E   E   D   A   E
           (Glo   - ri - a.) Yeah, yeah, yeah, yeah, yeah, so good.
                      D   A   E   D   A   E
           (Glo   - ri - a.) Alright.   Just so good.
                      D   A   E   D   A   E
           (Glo   - ri - a.) Alright. Yeah.
           | E   D   A | E   D   A |
</pre>

<pre>
Outro | E* D* A* D* | E* D* A* D* | E* D* A* D* | E
</pre>

Good Vibrations

Words and Music by
Brian Wilson and Mike Love

Melody:

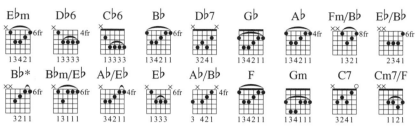

Verse 1

         Ebm   **Db6**
I, ____ I love the colorful clothes she wears,

         Cb6   **Bb**
And the way the sunlight plays upon her hair.

Ebm   **Db6**
I hear the sound of a gentle word,

        Cb6   **Bb**   **Db7**
On the wind that lifts her perfume through the air.

Chorus 1

        Gb
    I'm pickin' up good vibrations.

She's givin' me the excitations.

I'm pickin' up good vibrations.

She's givin' me the excitations.

Ab
    I'm pickin' up good vibrations.

She's givin' me the excitations.

Bb
    I'm pickin' up good vibrations.

She's givin' me the excitations.

	E♭m D♭6
Verse 2	Close my eyes, she's somehow closer now.

E♭m   **D♭6**

Verse 2

E♭m   **D♭6**
Close my eyes, she's somehow closer now.

C♭6   **B♭**
Softly smile, I know she must be kind.

E♭m   **D♭6**
When I look in her eyes

           C♭6   **B♭**   **D♭7**
She goes with me to a blossom room.

Chorus 2   *Repeat Chorus 1*

Bridge   ‖: **Fm/B♭**   **E♭/B♭** | **B♭***   **E♭/B♭**   :‖ *Play 5 times*

   Fm/B♭   **E♭/B♭**
(Oh,   my,

B♭*   **E♭/B♭**
My one ____ elation.)

   B♭m/E♭   **A♭/E♭**
I don't know where,

               E♭   **A♭/E♭**
But she sends __ me there.

B♭m/E♭   **A♭/E♭**   **E♭**   **A♭/B♭**
        My,   my one __ sensation.

Fm/B♭   **E♭/B♭**   **B♭***   **E♭/B♭**
Oh,   my,   my one elation.

Fm/B♭   **E♭/B♭**   **B♭***   **E♭/B♭**
My,   my,   my one...

Interlude | **F** | | **Gm** | **C7** |

	F					
Verse 3	Gotta keep those lovin' good					
	Gm		**C7**			
	Vibrations a happenin' with her.					

F

Gotta keep those lovin' good

Gm   **C7**

Vibrations a happenin' with her.

F

Gotta keep those lovin' good

Gm   **C7**

Vibrations a happenin' with her.

F			Gm	C7	
F			Cm7/F	N.C.	

B♭

Chorus 3   I'm pickin' up good vibrations.

She's givin' me the excitations.

A♭   **G♭**

Good, good, good, good vibrations.

G♭

Outro   Na, na, na, na, na,

Na, na, na.

A♭

Na, na, na, na, na,

Na, na, na.

B♭

Na, na, na, na, na,

Na, na, na.

A♭

Na, na, na, na, na,

Na, na, na.

‖: **A♭** | :‖ *Repeat and fade*

Heat of the Moment

Words and Music by
Geoffrey Downes and John Wetton

Tune down 1/2 step:
(low to high) Eb–Ab–Db–Gb–Bb–Eb

Melody:

I nev-er meant to

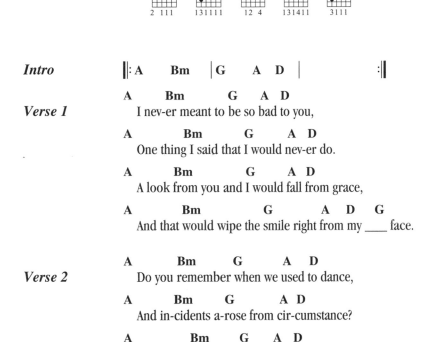

Intro ‖: A Bm | G A D | :‖

Verse 1

A   Bm   G   A D
I nev-er meant to be so bad to you,

A   Bm   G   A D
One thing I said that I would nev-er do.

A   Bm   G   A D
A look from you and I would fall from grace,

A   Bm   G   A   D G
And that would wipe the smile right from my ___ face.

Verse 2

A   Bm   G   A   D
Do you remember when we used to dance,

A   Bm   G   A D
And in-cidents a-rose from cir-cumstance?

A   Bm   G   A D
One thing led to an-other, we were young,

A   Bm   G   A   D G
And we would scream to-gether songs un - sung.

Chorus 1

               D   A   G   A
It was the heat ___ of the mo - ment

D   A   Bm   G
Tellin' you what   my heart ___ meant.

     D A   Bm   Em   Asus4   A
The heat of the mo - ment showed in your eyes.

Verse 3

A   Bm   G   A   D
  And now you find your-self in eight-y-two,

A   Bm   G   A   D
  The dis-co huff was on the charm for you.

A   Bm   G   A D
  You can concern your-self with big-ger things,

A   Bm   G   A   D   G
  You catch a pearl and ride the drag-ons ___ wings.

Chorus 2

               D A   G   A
'Cause it's the heat ___ of the mo - ment.

D   A   Bm   G
Heat of the mo - ment.

     D A   Bm
The heat of the mo - ment

Em   Asus4 A/G F#m7 Em7
Showed in your eyes.

Interlude

‖:B7sus4 | |Bm | :‖ *Play 3 times*
| B7sus4 | |G | |

Verse 4

A   Bm   G   A   D
And when your looks are gone and you're alone,

A   Bm   G A D
How man-y nights you sit be-side the phone?

A   Bm   G   A D
What were the things you wanted for yourself?

A   Bm   G   A   D G
Teenage ambitions you re-mem-ber ___ well.

Chorus 3

               D   A   G   A
It was the heat ___ of the mo - ment

D   A   Bm   G
Tellin' you what   your heart ___ meant.

     D A   Bm   Em   Asus4   A
The heat of the mo - ment showed in your eyes.

               D A   G   A
It was the heat ___ of the mo - ment.

D   A   Bm   G
Heat of the mo - ment.

D   A   Bm
Heat of the mo - ment

Em   Asus4 A/G F#m7 Em7
Showed in your eyes.

Outro

| N.C. | |

‖: D A | G A | D A | Bm G |

| D A/C# | Bm Em | Asus4 | A   :‖ *Repeat and fade*

Green-Eyed Lady

Words and Music by Jerry Corbetta,
J.C. Phillips and David Riordan

Melody:

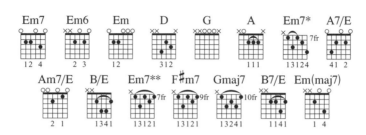

Intro

N.C.		Em7 Em6	N.C.			Em7 Em
N.C.		Em D	G A	Em		
		Em7*		‖: N.C.	:‖	*Play 8 times*

Verse 1

Em7   A7/E
Green-eyed lady, lovely la - dy,

   Am7/E   Em7
Strolling slowly towards the sun.

        A7/E
Green-eyed lady, ocean la - dy,

   Am7/E   Em7
Soothing ev'ry ragging wave that comes.

        A7/E
Green-eyed lady, passions la - dy,

   Am7/E   Em7
Dressed in love, she lives for life to be.

       A7/E
Green-eyed lady feels life,

   Am7/E   Em7 B/E
I never see setting suns and lonely lovers free.

Organ Solo	‖:Em7** F#m7 Gmaj7 |	F#m7 Em7** |	
	| F#m7 Gmaj7 |	F#m7 :‖	*Play 5 times*

Guitar Solo	| N.C.(Em7) |	|	|
	| |	|	|
	| (B/E) |	|	|
	| | (B7/E) |	|	|
	| Em(maj7) |	|	|

Interlude	| N.C. |	|	| Am7/E |	|
	| | Em7 |	|	|

Verse 2

```
Em7                          A7/E
  Green-eyed lady, wind swept la - dy,

        Am7/E             Em7
Rules the night, the waves, the sand.

                      A7/E
Green-eyed lady, ocean la - dy,

        Am7/E           Em7
Child of na - ture, friend of man.

                      A7/E
Green-eyed lady, passions lady,

        Am7/E                 Em7
Dressed in love, she lives for life to be.

                      A7/E
Green-eyed lady feels life,

             Am7/E                   Em7
I never see setting suns and lonely lovers free.
```

Outro	| Em7 |	| A7/E |	|
	| Am7/E |	| Em7 |	| *Fade out*

Hot Blooded

Words and Music by
Mick Jones and Lou Gramm

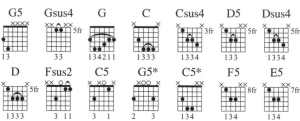

Intro
‖: G5   :‖ *Play 4 times*
| Gsus4   G | C   Csus4 |
| G5   Gsus4   G | C   Csus4 |

Chorus 1
      G5 Gsus4   G   C   Csus4
Well, I'm   hot blood-ed, check it and see.
G5 Gsus4 G   C   Csus4
    I got a fe-ver of a hundred and three.
G5 Gsus4   G   C   Csus4
    Come on, ba-by, do you do more than dance?
D5   Dsus4   D   Dsus4   D
    I'm hot blood-ed. I'm hot blood-ed.

Verse 1
| G5* | Fsus2 |
C5   G5*
You don't have to read my mind
Fsus2   C5   G5*
    To know what I have in mind.
Fsus2   C5   G5*
    Honey, you ought to know.
Fsus2   C5   G5*
     Now, you move so fine,
Fsus2   C5   G5*
     Let me lay it on the line.
Fsus2   C5 G5*
      I   wanna know what you're
Fsus2 C5   G5*   Fsus2   C5
Doin'   after the show.

Pre-Chorus 1

        C5* D5   C5* D5
Now it's up   to you.

F5   **C5***   **D5 C5* D5**   **E5 C5***
We can make a secret ren-dez - vous.

          D5 C5* D5
Just me and you,

F5   **C5***   **D5 C5* D5**   **N.C.**
I'll show you lovin' ____ like you never knew.

Chorus 2

               G5 Gsus4   G C   **Csus4**
That's why I'm   hot blood-ed, check it and see.

G5 Gsus4 G   **C**   **Csus4**
     I got a fe-ver of a hundred and three.

G5 Gsus4   **G**   **C**   **Csus4**
     Come on, ba-by, do you do more than dance?

D5 Dsus4   **D**   **Dsus4**   **D**
     I'm hot blood-ed. I'm hot blood-ed.

Verse 2

| **G5*** | **Fsus2**

C5   **G5***
    If it feels ____ all right,

Fsus2 C5   **G5***
    Maybe you can   stay all night.

Fsus2   **C5**   **G5***
    Should I ____ leave you my key?

Fsus2 C5   **G5***
    But you've got to give me a sign.

Fsus2   **C5 G5***
    Come on, girl, some kind of sign.

Fsus2   **C5**   **G5***
    Tell me,   are you   hot, mama?

Fsus2   **C5**   **G5*** **Fsus2 C5**
    You sure look that way to me.

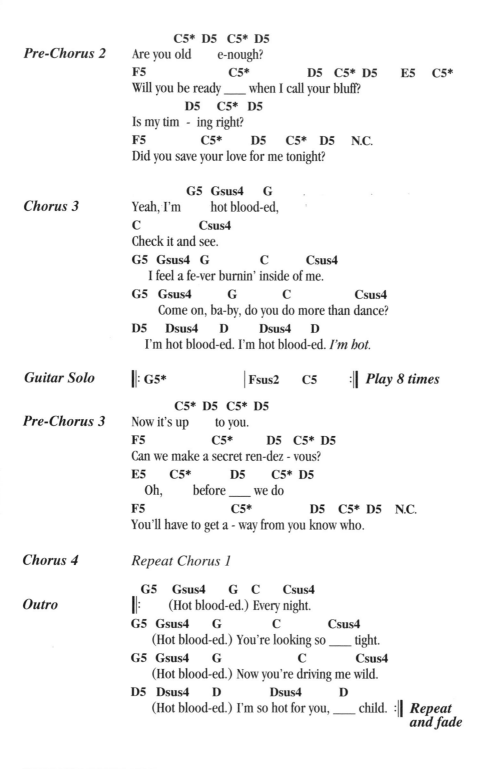

Pre-Chorus 2

        C5* D5 C5* D5
Are you old   e-nough?

F5   C5*   D5 C5* D5   E5   C5*
Will you be ready ___ when I call your bluff?

           D5 C5* D5
Is my tim - ing right?

F5   C5*   D5   C5* D5   N.C.
Did you save your love for me tonight?

Chorus 3

          G5 Gsus4   G
Yeah, I'm   hot blood-ed,

C   Csus4
Check it and see.

G5 Gsus4 G   C   Csus4
  I feel a fe-ver burnin' inside of me.

G5 Gsus4   G   C   Csus4
   Come on, ba-by, do you do more than dance?

D5 Dsus4   D   Dsus4   D
   I'm hot blood-ed. I'm hot blood-ed. *I'm hot.*

Guitar Solo

‖: G5* |Fsus2   C5   :‖ *Play 8 times*

Pre-Chorus 3

          C5* D5 C5* D5
Now it's up   to you.

F5   C5*   D5 C5* D5
Can we make a secret ren-dez - vous?

E5   C5*   D5   C5* D5
  Oh,   before ___ we do

F5   C5*   D5 C5* D5 N.C.
You'll have to get a - way from you know who.

Chorus 4   *Repeat Chorus 1*

Outro

    G5   Gsus4   G   C   Csus4
‖:   (Hot blood-ed.) Every night.

G5 Gsus4   G   C   Csus4
   (Hot blood-ed.) You're looking so ___ tight.

G5 Gsus4   G   C   Csus4
   (Hot blood-ed.) Now you're driving me wild.

D5 Dsus4   D   Dsus4   D
   (Hot blood-ed.) I'm so hot for you, ___ child. :‖ *Repeat*
                                               and fade

I Love Rock 'n Roll

Words and Music by
Alan Merrill and Jake Hooker

Melody:

I saw him danc-in' there, _ by the rec-ord ma - chine.

E5   A5   B5   E7

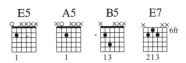

Intro

| E5 | | A5 | B5 | E5 | | |
| A5 | B5 A5 | E5 | | | |

Verse 1

    E5
I saw him dancin' there, by the record machine.

             B5
I knew he must have been about seven-teen.

  A5   **B5** **E5**   **A5**
The beat was goin' strong, ___ playin' my favorite song.

And I could tell it wouldn't be long

        N.C.
Till he was with me, yeah, me.

And I could tell it wouldn't be long

      B5
Till he was with me, yeah, me. Singin',

Chorus 1

E5
I love rock 'n' roll,

A5   B5
So put another dime in the jukebox, baby.

E5
I love rock 'n' roll,

A5   B5   E5
So come and take your time and dance with me.   Ow!

Verse 2

E5
He smiled, so I got up and asked for his name.

B5
"That don't matter," he said, "'Cause it's all the same."

A5   B5   E5   A5
I said, "Can I take ya home ___ where we can be a-lone?"

N.C.
And next, we were movin' on, he was with me, yeah, me.

B5
Next, we were movin' on, he was with me, yeah, me. Singin',

Chorus 2   *Repeat Chorus 1*

Guitar Solo | E5 | E7 | E5 | B5 |

Pre-Chorus

A5   B5   E5   A5
Said, "Can I take ya home ___ where we can be a-lone?"

Next, we were movin' on, he was with me, yeah, me.

N.C.
And we'll be movin' on, and singin' that same old song,

Yeah, with me, singin',

Chorus 3

N.C.
I love rock 'n' roll,

So put another dime in the jukebox, baby.

I love rock 'n' roll,

So come and take your time and dance with me.

Outro

E5
‖: I love rock 'n' roll,

  A5   **B5**
So put another dime in the jukebox, baby.

E5
I love rock 'n' roll,

  A5   **B5**
So come and take your time and dance with... :‖ *Play 3 times*

E5
I love rock 'n' roll,

  A5   **B5**
So put another dime in the jukebox, baby.

E5
I love rock 'n' roll,

  A5   **B5**   **E5**
So come and take your time and dance with me.

I Fought the Law

Words and Music by Sonny Curtis

A break - in' __ rocks in the hot sun.

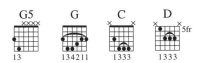

| G5 | G | C | D |
| 13 | 134211 | 1333 | 1333 |

Intro |G5 | |G |C   D |
|G |D G D G |

Verse 1
```
        G                C   G
A breakin' rocks in the    hot sun.

G                 C   G
I fought the law and the    law won.

                 D   G
I fought the law and the    law won.
```
|C   D |G |D G D G |

Verse 2
```
        G              C   G
I miss my baby and the    good fun.

G                 C   G
I fought the law and the    law won.

                 D   G
I fought the law and the    law won.
```
|C   D |G |D G D G |

Bridge 1

      C
I left my baby and I feel so bad.

      G
I guess my race is run.

        C
Well, she's the best girl I ever had.

G   **C**   **G**
I fought the law and the   law won.

                 D   **G**
I fought the law and the   law won.

| C | D | G | D | G | D | G |

Solo

C		G		
C		G	C	G
	D	G		

Verse 3

G   **C**   **G**
Robbin' people with a   six gun.

G   **C**   **G**
I fought the law and the   law won.

                 D   **G**
I fought the law and the   law won.

Verse 4   ***Repeat Verse 2***

Bridge 2   ***Repeat Bridge 1***

I Want You to Want Me

Words and Music by Rick Nielsen

A	F#m	A/E	D	B7	G	E	D7	G5

Verse 1

      A
I want you to want me.

   F#m   **A/E**
I need you to need me.

      D
I'd love you to love me.

       A
I'm beggin' you to beg me.

Verse 2

   F#m   **A/E**
I want you to want me.

    D
I need you to need me.

    A
I'd love you to love me.

Bridge 1

     F#m   **B7**
I'll shine up my old brown shoes.

    G   **A**
I'll put on a brand new shirt.

     F#m   **B7**
I'll get home early from work

      G   **F#m**
If you say that you love__ me.

	A E
Chorus 1	Didn't I, didn't I, didn't I see you cryin'?

(Cryin', cryin'.)

   F#m   D7
Oh, didn't I, didn't I, didn't I see you cryin'?

(Cryin', cryin'.)

A
Feelin' all alone without a friend

                       E
You know you feel like dyin'.

(Dyin', dyin'.)

   F#m   D7
Oh, didn't I, didn't I, didn't I see you cryin'?

(Cryin', cryin'.)

Verse 3   **Repeat Verse 1**

                 A   E
Chorus 2   Didn't I, didn't I, didn't I see you cryin'?

(Cryin', cryin'.)

   F#m   D7
Oh, didn't I, didn't I, didn't I see you cryin'?

(Cryin', cryin'.)

A
Feelin' all alone without a friend

                       E
You know you feel like dyin'.

(Dyin', dyin'.)

   F#m   D7
Oh, didn't I, didn't I, didn't I see you cryin'? Oh.

Solo 1 | A | | E | | |
              | F#m | | D7 | | |

Chorus 3
              A
              Feelin' all alone without a friend

                                  E
              You know you feel like dyin'.

              (Dyin', dyin'.)

                 F#m   D7
              Oh, didn't I, didn't I, didn't I see you cryin'? Oh.

Solo 2 | A | | E | | |
              | F#m | | D7 | | |

Verse 4   **Repeat Verse 1**

Outro
                 N.C.
              ‖: I want you to want me. :‖ *Play 4 times*

              | A | | | |
              | G5 | D | A | |

It's Only Love

Words and Music by
Bryan Adams and Jim Vallance

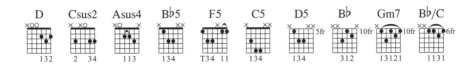

Intro

‖: D   Csus2 |Asus4   B♭5 N.C. |

|F5 | :‖ *Play 3 times*

Verse 1

                   D   Csus2

Bryan Adams: When the feelin' is ended,

       Asus4   B♭5 N.C.

There ain't no use pretend - in'.

       F5

Don't ya wor - ry, well, it's only love.

         D   Csus2

When your world has been shattered,

     Asus4   B♭5   N.C.

Ain't nothin' else matters.

      F5

It ain't o - ver, well, it's only love, and that's all, yeah.

Guitar Solo 1

|D   Csus2 |Asus4   B♭5 N.C. |

|F5 | |

Verse 2

                D   Csus2
Tina Turner: Yeah, if your heart has been broken,

       Asus4   Bb5   N.C.
Hard words have been spoken,

        F5
It ain't eas - y, but it's only love.

          D   Csus2
And if your life ain't worth livin'

        Asus4   Bb5 N.C.
And you're ready to give in,

        F5
Just remem - ber that it's only love. Oh.

Guitar Solo 2

| D   Csus2 | Asus4   Bb5 N.C. |
| F5 | |

                       Turner: Ah,

| D   Csus2 | Asus4   Bb5 N.C. |
  yeah.   Only
| F5 | |
  love.   *Adams:* Yeah.

Bridge

        C5   D5
Both: You can live without the ag - gravation.

Bb   Gm7
  Ya gotta wanna win,   ya gotta wanna win.

C5   D5
  You keep lookin' back in desperation

              Bb/C
Over and over and over again.

Interlude | D   Csus2 |Asus4   Bb5 N.C. |

| F5 | |

        D   Csus2   Asus4   Bb5

Adams: Yeah, oh, yeah.

N.C.   F5

It's only love, ___ baby. *Turner:* Oh, yeah. *Adams:* Oh, yeah.

D   Csus2 Asus4   Bb5   N.C.   F5

     Oo, ___ ba - by, baby, it's only love, love, love.

Turner: Love, love, love.

                 D   Csus2

Verse 3   *Adams:* When your world is shattered,

          Asus4   Bb5

Ain't nothin' else matters.

N.C.   F5

Well, it ain't o - ver, it's only love.

       D   Csus2

If your life ain't worth livin'

      Asus4   Bb5 N.C.

And you're ready to give in,

         F5

Just remem - ber that it's only love, yeah, that's all.

Outro | D   Csus2 |Asus4   Bb5 N.C. |

| F5 | |

   Turner: Oh, love, love, yeah.

| D   Csus2 |Asus4   Bb5 N.C. |

| F5 | |

            Adams: Hey. Yeah.

| D   Csus2 |Asus4   Bb5 N.C. |
               Yeah, it ain't

| F5 | |

 easy, baby. It's only love and that's all.

La Grange

Words and Music by Billy F Gibbons,
Dusty Hill and Frank Beard

Ru - mor spread-in' 'round,

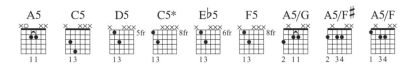

Intro | A5 | | | | |

Rumor spreadin' 'round, in that Texas town,

'Bout that shack outside La Grange.

And you know what I'm talkin' about.

Just let me know if you wanna go

To that home out on the range.

                                          N.C.
They gotta lotta nice girls.

A5   **C5 D5 A5**   **C5 D5**
  Have mercy.

A5   **C5 D5 A5**
  A haw, haw, haw, haw.   A haw,   a haw, haw, haw.

Verse

       C5 D5   A5   C5 D5   A5
Well, I hear it's fine, ___ if you got the time

C5 D5 A5   C5 D5 A5
And the ten to get your-self in ___ a, hmm, hmm.

       C5   D5 A5   C5 D5   A5
And I hear it's tight most ever-y night,

C5   D5 A5   C5 D5 A5
 But now ___ I might be mis-taken.

             N.C.
Hmm, hmm, hmm.

Guitar Solo ‖: C5* | E♭5 F5 :‖ *Play 16 times*

Interlude ‖: A5/G | A5/F♯ | A5/F | A5   :‖
            | A5 | | |
            | | | N.C. |

Outro ‖: A5 | C5 D5 :‖ *Repeat and fade*

L.A. Woman

Words and Music
by The Doors

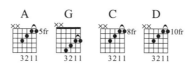

Intro ‖: A :‖ *Play 33 times*

Verse 1

       A
Well, I just got into town about an hour ago,

Took a look around, see which way the wind blow,

With a little girl in a Hollywood bungalow.

Are you a lucky little lady in the city of light,

Or just another lost angel?

           G   A
City of night, ___ city of night.

           G   A
City of night, ___ city of night.   Whoa! Come on!

Guitar Solo ‖: A | :‖ *Play 12 times*

Verse 2

A
L.A. woman, L.A. woman.

L.A. woman Sunday afternoon.

L.A. woman Sunday afternoon.

L.A. woman Sunday afternoon,
                                        G
Drive through your suburbs into your blues.
          A
Into your blues. Yeah!
          G   A
Into your blue, blue, blue, into your blues. Oh, yeah!

Piano Solo   ‖: A | :‖ *Play 8 times*

Interlude 1   ‖: A   G | A   G   :‖ *Play 4 times*

              A   G   A   G   A G A G
Bridge 1   I see your __ hair is burn-ing,
              A   G   A   G   A G A G
              Hills are __ filled with fire.
                  A   G   A   G   A   G A G
              If they say I __ never loved you,
                A   G   A G   A   G A G
              You know they __ are a li - ar.
              A   G   A   G   A G   A   G
              Drivin' down your freeway,
              A   G   A   G   A   G A G
              Midnight ___ alleys roam.
              A
              Cops in cars, the topless bars,
                                        G   A
              Never saw a woman so a-lone, so alone.
                    G   A
              So a-lone, so alone.

              Motel money, murder madness,

              A, change the mood from glad to sadness.

| *Interlude 2* | ‖: N.C.(Am)   │   :‖ *Play 6 times* |

                          N.C.(Am)

Bridge 2   Mister Mojo risin'. Mister Mojo risin'.

                        Mister Mojo risin'. Mister Mojo risin'.

                        Gotta keep on risin'.

                        Mister Mojo risin'. Mister Mojo risin'.

                        Mojo risin'. Got my Mojo risin'.

                        Mister Mojo risin'. Gotta keep on risin'.

                        Risin', risin'. Gon' ride in, ride in.

                        Gonna ride in, ride in. I gotta ride in, ride in.

                        Babe, ride in, ride in.

                            C   **D**

                        I gotta, whoa, yeah. Right. Oh. Yeah.

                        │ **A**   │   │   │   │

Verse 3   *Repeat Verse 1*

Outro   ‖: A   │   :‖ *Repeat and fade*
                                                                  (w/voc. ad lib.)

Love Is a Battlefield

Words and Music by
Mike Chapman and Holly Knight

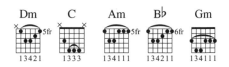

Dm   C   Am   B♭   Gm

Intro
‖: Dm | C | Am B♭ | :‖
| Dm | C | Am B♭ | |
(We are young.)   (We are young.)

Chorus 1

Dm   C
We are young.

Am   B♭   Dm C
Heartache to heartache we stand.

Am   B♭   Dm C
No promis-es no demands.

Am   B♭
Love is a battlefield.

Dm   C
Whoa, whoa, whoa, whoa, whoa, whoa,

             Am B♭   Dm   C
Whoa, whoa, whoa.   We are strong.

Am   B♭   Dm C
No one can tell us we're wrong.

Am   B♭   Dm C
Searching our hearts for so long,

Am   B♭
Both of us knowing love is a battlefield.

Interlude 1
| Dm | | C | |
| B♭ | | | | |

                        Dm   **C**
Verse 1   You're begging me to go, then making me stay.

                B♭   **Gm**
                  Why do you hurt me so ___ bad?

                        Dm   **C**
                It would help me to know, do I stand in your way

                B♭   **Gm**
                  Or am I the best thing you've ___ had.

                  Dm   **C**
                Be-lieve me, believe me, I can't tell you why,

                        B♭
                But I'm trapped by your love

                        Gm
                And I'm chained to your side.

                        Dm   **C**
Chorus 2   We are young.

                Am   **B♭**   **Dm**   **C**
                Heartache to heartache we stand.

                Am   **B♭**   **Dm** **C**
                No promis-es, no demands.

                Am   **B♭**   **Dm** **C** **Am** **B♭**
                Love is a battlefield.

                        Dm   **C**
                We are strong.

                Am   **B♭**   **Dm**   **C**
                No one can tell us we're wrong.

                Am   **B♭**   **Dm**   **C**
                Searching our hearts for so long,

                Am   **B♭**
                Both of us knowing love is a battlefield.

Interlude 2	*Repeat Interlude 1*

                        Dm   **C**

Verse 2   When I'm losing control, will you turn me away,

                    B♭   **Gm**

                    Or touch me deep inside?

                      Dm   **C**

                    And if all this gets old, will it still feel the same?

                    B♭   **Gm**

                    There's no way this will die.

                      Dm   **C**

                    But if we get much closer, I could lose control.

                      B♭   **Gm**

                    And if your heart surrenders, you'll need me to hold.

Chorus 3	*Repeat Chorus 2*

Interlude 3   ‖: Dm | | C | |

                    | B♭ | | | :‖

Guitar Solo	*Repeat Interlude 3*
Outro	*Repeat Chorus 2 till fade*

Layla

Words and Music by
Eric Clapton and Jim Gordon

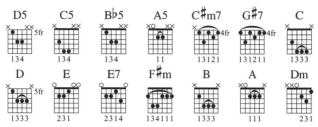

D5	C5	Bb5	A5	C#m7	G#7	C

D	E	E7	F#m	B	A	Dm

Intro ‖: **D5 C5 Bb5** | **C5 D5** :‖ *Play 5 times*
          | **C5 Bb5** | **C5   A5 C5** |

Verse 1
C#m7   **G#7**
What will you do when you get lone - ly?

C#m7   C   D   E   E7
No one waiting by your __ side.

F#m   B   E   A
You've been runnin', hidin' much too long.

F#m   B   E
You know it's just your foolish pride.

Chorus 1
A D5 C5 Bb5
Layla,

C5   D5
Got me on my knees.

        C5 Bb5
Layla,

C5   D5
Beggin' dar-lin', please.

        C5 Bb5
Layla,

C5   D5   **C5 Bb5 C5 A5 C5**
Darlin', won't you ease my worried mind?

Verse 2

C#m7   G#7
Tried to give you conso-lation,

C#m7   C   D   E   E7
Your old man had let you down.

F#m   B   E   A
Like a fool, I fell in love with you.

F#m   B   E
You turned my whole world upside down.

Chorus 2

A D5 C5 Bb5
Layla,

C5   D5
Got me on my knees.

C5 Bb5
Layla,

C5   D5
Beggin' dar-lin', please.

C5 Bb5
Layla,

C5   D5   C5 Bb5   C5 A5 C5
Darlin', won't you ease my worried mind?

Verse 3

C#m7   G#7
Make the best of the situ-ation,

C#m7   C   D   E   E7
Before I fin'ly go in-sane.

F#m   B   E   A
Please don't say we'll never find a way.

F#m   B   E
Tell me all my love's in vain.

Chorus 3

A D5 C5 Bb5
Layla,

C5   D5
Got me on my knees.

      C5 Bb5
Layla,

C5   D5
Beggin' dar-lin', please.

      C5 Bb5
Layla,

C5   D5   C5 Bb5 C5 D5
Darlin', won't you ease my worried mind?

Chorus 4	**D5 C5 B♭5** Layla,
	C5 D5 Got me on my knees.
	C5 B♭5 Layla,
	C5 D5 Beggin' dar-lin', please.
	C5 B♭5 Layla,
	C5 D5 C5 B♭5 C5 D5 Darlin', won't you ease my worried mind?

Guitar Solo   ‖: **D5   C5   B♭5** | **C5   D5**   :‖ *Play 8 times*

Chorus 5   *Repeat Chorus 4*

Chorus 6	**D5 C5 B♭5** Layla,
	C5 D5 Got me on my knees.
	C5 B♭5 Layla,
	C5 D5 Beggin' dar-lin', please.
	C5 B♭5 Layla,
	C **Dm** Darlin', won't you ease my worried mind?

Lights

Words and Music by
Steve Perry and Neal Schon

Melody:

When the   lights _   go down

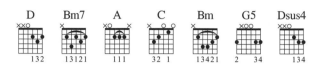

D   Bm7   A   C   Bm   G5   Dsus4

| | | | | | | |
132   13121   111   32 1   13421   2 34   134

Intro

| D | Bm7 | D | A | |
| Bm7 | C | D | | |

Verse 1

       D   **Bm**   **C**
When the lights go down in the city

       D   **Bm** **C**
And the sun shines on the bay,

      D   **Bm**   **C**
Oo, I wanna be there ____ in my __ city.

   Bm C D
Oh. Oh, ____ oh.

Verse 2

D   **Bm**   **C**
So you think you're __ lonely.

D   **Bm**   **C**
Well, my friend, I'm __ lonely too.

D   **Bm**   **C**
I want to get back to my city by the bay.

Bm   **C D**
Whoa, oh, oh.

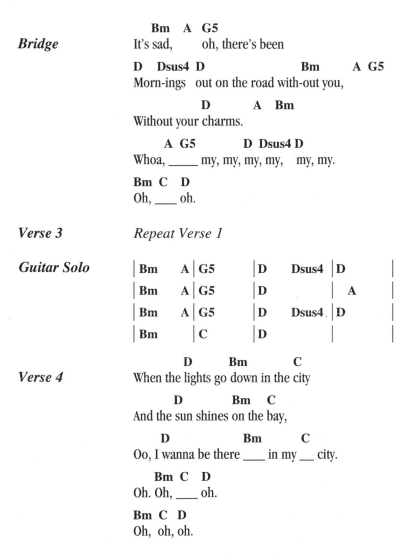

Bridge

      Bm   A G5
It's sad,   oh, there's been

D   Dsus4 D   Bm   A G5
Morn-ings   out on the road with-out you,

            D   A   Bm
Without your charms.

       A G5   D Dsus4 D
Whoa, _____ my, my, my, my,   my, my.

Bm C   D
Oh, ___ oh.

Verse 3   *Repeat Verse 1*

Guitar Solo

Bm	A	G5	D	Dsus4	D	
Bm	A	G5	D		A	
Bm	A	G5	D	Dsus4	D	
Bm		C	D			

          D   Bm   C
Verse 4   When the lights go down in the city

          D   Bm   C
And the sun shines on the bay,

        D   Bm   C
Oo, I wanna be there ___ in my __ city.

      Bm C   D
Oh. Oh, ___ oh.

Bm C   D
Oh, oh, oh.

Money

Words and Music
by Roger Waters

Mon-ey,   ah, get a - way.

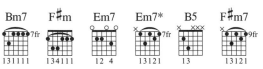

Bm7   F#m   Em7   Em7*   B5   F#m7

Intro   ‖: **Bm7** | :‖ *Play 4 times*

                 Bm7
Verse 1   Money, ah, get away.

                 You get a good job with more pay and you're okay.

                 Money, it's a gas.

                 Grab that cash with both hands and make a stash.
                 F#m
                 New car, caviar, four star daydream.

                 Em7   **Bm7**
                 Think I'll buy me a football ____ team.

                 Bm7
Verse 2   Money, well, get back.

                 I'm all right, Jack, keep your hands off of my stack.

                 Money, it's a hit.

                 Ah, don't give me that do goody good bullshit.
                     F#m   **Em7**
                 I'm in the high fidelity first class traveling set,

                         Bm7
                 And I think I need a Lear ____ jet.

Sax Solo	‖:**Bm7** |	|	|	:‖
	|**Em7*** |	|	|	|
	|**Bm7** |	|	|	|
	|**F#m** |	|**Em7**	|**B5**	|
	| |			

Guitar Solo	‖:**Bm7** |	|	|	:‖
	|**Em7*** |	|	|	|
	|**Bm7** |	|	|	|
	|**F#m7** |	|**N.C.**	|	|
	‖:**Bm7** |	|	|	:‖ *Play 3 times*
	|**Em7*** |	|	|	|
	|**Bm7** |	|	|	|
	|**F#m7** |	|**N.C.**	|	|
	‖:**Bm7** |	|	|	:‖ *Play 3 times*
	|**Em7*** |	|	|	|
	|**Bm7** |	|	|	|
	|**F#m7** |	|**N.C.**	|	|
	|**Bm7** |	|		

Bm7

Verse 3

Money, it's a crime.

Share it fairly but don't take a slice of my pie.

Money, so they say,

Is the root of all evil today.

F#m   **Em7**
But if you ask for a rise it's no sur-prise

                              Bm7
That they're giving none away,

Away, away, 'way, away, away, away, away.

Outro   ‖:**Bm7** \| :‖ *Repeat and fade (w/voc. ad lib.)*

Money for Nothing

Words and Music by
Mark Knopfler and Sting

Melody:

I want my, _____

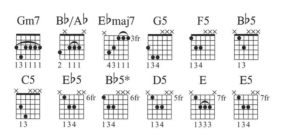

Gm7 Bb/Ab Ebmaj7 G5 F5 Bb5
C5 Eb5 Bb5* D5 E E5

Prelude

Gm7
I want my, I want my M.T.V.

I want my, I want my M.T.V.

         Bb/Ab
I want my M.T.V.

            Ebmaj7
I want my, I want my M.T.V.

            Gm7 G5 F5 G5 F5
I want my, I want my M.T.V.

Intro

‖: G5 | | | Bb5 C5 |

| G5 | | | F5 G5 :‖

Verse 1

G5

Now, look at them yo-yos, that's the way you do it,

Bb5 C5

You play the guitar on the M.T. V.

G5

That ain't workin', that's the way you do it,

F5   G5

Money for nothin' and your chicks for free.

Now, that ain't workin', that's the way you do it,

Bb5   C5

Let me tell ya them guys ain't dumb.

G5

You maybe get a blister on your little finger,

F5   G5

Maybe get a blister on your ___ thumb.

Chorus 1

Eb5   Bb5*

We gotta install microwave ovens,

Eb5   F5   G5

Custom kitchen de-liveries.

We gotta move these refrigerators,

C5   D5   E

We gotta move these color T.V.'s.   Ow!

Verse 2

G5
    See the little faggot with the earring and the makeup?

        Bb5   C5
Yeah, buddy, that's his own hair.

G5
    That little faggot got his own jet airplane.

           F5   G5
That little faggot, he's a millionaire.

Chorus 2   *Repeat Chorus 1*

Interlude 1
G5			
Bb5 C5	G5		
	F5 G5	

Chorus 3

Eb5   Bb5*
    (Gotta install microwave ovens,

Eb5   F5
    Custom kitchen de-liveries.)

G5
We gotta move these refrigerators.

C5   D5   E5
    (We gotta move these color T.V.'s.)

Look at ya, look here.

                        G5
Verse 3   I shoulda learned to play the guitar,
                              Bb5   C5
                    I shoulda learned to play them drums.

                              G5
                    Look at that mama, she got it.

                                           F5   G5
                    Stickin' in the camera, man, we could have some fun.

                    And he's up there. What's that? Hawaiian noises?
                                        Bb5   C5
                    He's bangin' on the bongos like a chimpan-zee.

                              G5
                    Oh, that ain't workin', that's the way you do it,

                                           F5   G5
                    Get your money for nothin', get your chicks for free.

Chorus 4   *Repeat Chorus 1*

Interlude 2 | **G5** | | |
                    | **Bb5   C5** | **G5** | |
                    | | **F5**   **G5** |
                                      Listen here.

                              G5
Verse 4   Now,   that ain't working, that's the way you do it,
                                        Bb5   C5
                    You play the guitar on the M.T.V.

                    G5
                      That ain't workin', that's the way you do it,

                                        F5   G5
                    Money for nothin' and your chicks for free.

                                        Bb5   C5
                    Money for nothin', chicks for free.

Outro   ‖: **G5** | | **F5**   **G5** |
                    | | | **Bb5** **C5** :‖   ***Repeat and fade***
                                                                        (w/voc. ad lib.)

Mony, Mony

Words and Music by Bobby Bloom,
Tommy James, Ritchie Cordell and Bo Gentry

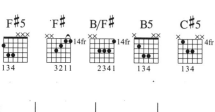

Intro | F#5 | | | |

Verse 1

         F#   **B/F# F#**
Here ___ she comes now saying, "mony, mony."

                                B/F# F#
Shoot 'em down, turn around, come on, mony.

                             B/F# F#
Hey, she give me love and I feel all right now.

         F#5
Yeah! You gotta toss and turn and feel all right,

      B5   **C#5**
And I feel ___ all right, I say yeah, ___(Yeah,) yeah, (yeah,)

Yeah, (Yeah.) yeah, (Yeah.) yeah.

Chorus 1

             F#5
'Cause you make me feel (Like a pony.) so good,

(Like a pony.) so good, (Like a pony.) so good,

           B5
(Mony, mony.) so fine, ___ (Mony, mony.) so fine,

(Mony, mony.) it's so fine. (Mony, mony.) Well, I feel all right.

            C#5
(Mony, mony.) I say yeah, ___ (Yeah.) yeah, (Yeah.) yeah, (Yeah.)

Yeah, (Yeah.) yeah, (Yeah.) yeah. (Yeah.)

Interlude 1

| N.C. | | | | |
| F#5 | B5 | F#5 | B5 | |

Bridge

      B5   F#5   B5

‖:   (Oo, I love you, mony, mo-mo-mo - ny

                F#5   B5

Oo, I love you, mony, mo-mo-mo - ny.) :‖ *Play 4 times*

            C#5

Say yeah, ___ (Yeah.) yeah, (Yeah.) yeah, (Yeah.) yeah, (Yeah.)

Yeah, (Yeah.) yeah. (Yeah.)

Chorus 2

F#5

Come on. Come on. Come on. Come on.

B5

   Come on, come on. Come on, come on.

Come on, come on, feel all right.

        C#5

I say yeah, ___ (Yeah.) yeah, (Yeah.) yeah, (Yeah.) yeah, (Yeah.)

Yeah, (Yeah.) yeah. (Yeah.)

Interlude 2

| F#5 | | | | |

Verse 2

     F#   B/F# F#

Wake ___ it, shake it, mony, mony.

                                    B/F# F#

Shotgun dead and a come on, mony.

                                     B/F# F#

Don't stop cookin' 'cause I feel all right now.

       F#5

Hey! But don't stop now, come on, mony,

     B5

Come ___ on, yeah.

        C#5

I say yeah, ___ (Yeah.) yeah, (Yeah.) yeah, (Yeah.) yeah, (Yeah.)

Yeah. (Yeah.)

Chorus 3

$$F^{\sharp}5$$

'Cause you make me feel (Like a pony.) so good,

(Like a pony.) so good, (Like a pony.) Well, I feel all right.

$$B5$$

(Mony, mony.)   You so fine, (Mony, mony.) you so fine,

(Mony, mony.) you so fine. (Mony, mony.) I will be all right.

$$C^{\sharp}5$$

(Mony, mony.) I say yeah, ___ (Yeah.) yeah, (Yeah.) yeah, (Yeah.)

$$F^{\sharp}5$$

Yeah, (yeah.) yeah, I wanna   ride your pony, ride your pony,

$$B5$$

Ride your pony. Come on, come on. (Come on!)

Come on, mony. Feel all right.

$$C^{\sharp}5$$

I say yeah, ___ (Yeah.) yeah, (Yeah.) yeah, (Yeah.)

Yeah, (Yeah.) yeah.

Chorus 4

$$F^{\sharp}5$$

'Cause you make me feel (Like a pony.) so good,

(Like a pony.) so good, (Like a pony.) so good.

$$B5$$

(Like a pony.)   Come on! (Mony, mony.) Yeah, all right.

(Mony, mony. Mony, mony.) Well, I feel so good.

$$C^{\sharp}5$$

(Mony, mony.) I say yeah, ___ (Yeah.) yeah, (Yeah.) yeah, (Yeah.)

Yeah. (Yeah.)   *Fade out*

New Kid in Town

Words and Music by John David Souther,
Don Henley and Glenn Frey

Melody:

There's talk on the street, —

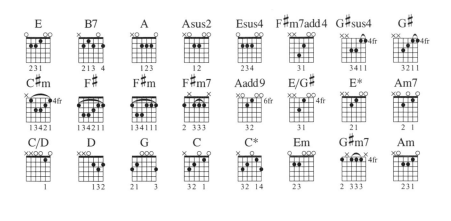

Intro

| E | | | B7 | | |
| A   Asus2 | B7 | E | | |

Verse 1

                                                B7
There's talk on the street, it sounds so famil - iar.

Asus2   **B7**   **E**   **Esus4 E**
  Great expecta - tions, ev'rybody's watching you.

                                B7
People you meet, they all seem to know ____ you.

Asus2   **B7**
  Even your old ____ friends

                    E   **F#m7add4 G#sus4 G#**
Treat you like you're some - thing new.

Chorus 1

C#m   F# C#m   F#
Johnny come late - ly,   the new kid in town.

C#m   F#   F#m   B7
Ev'rybody loves you.   So don't let them down.

Verse 2

E   F#m7 B7   F#m7 B7
You look in her eyes, the music be-gins to play.

A Asus2   B7   E
Hopeless roman - tics, here we go a-gain.

                           A   B7
But after a while you're looking the other way.

A B7   A   Asus2 B7
It's those   rest - less   hearts

         E   F#m7add4 G#sus4 G#
That never mend.

Chorus 2

       C#m   F# C#m   F#
Oh,   Johnny come late - ly,   the new kid in town.

C#m   F#   F#m   B7
Will she still love you   when you're not a-round?

Guitar Solo

E		B7		
Asus2	B7	E	
Aadd9	E/G#	F#m7add4	E*	

Interlude

B7   E
There's so many things you should have told her,

B7   C#m
But night after night you're willin' to hold her,

     F#   Am7   C/D D
Just hold her. Tears on your shoul - der.

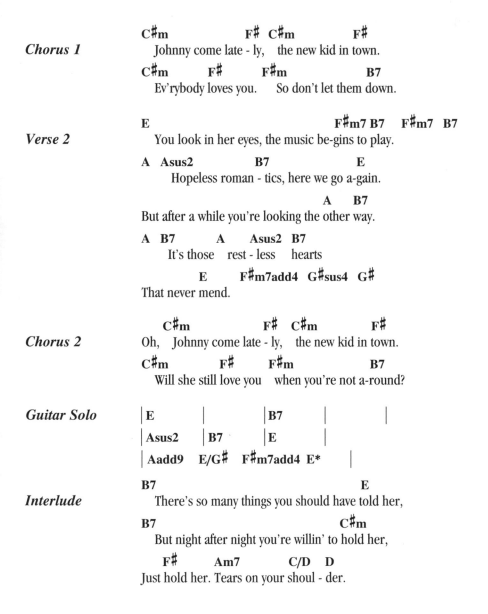

Verse 3

G
There's talk on the street,
       C D C D
It's there to remind ___ you.
C*   D   G D C
It doesn't really matter which side you're on.
G
You're walking away
         C D C D
And they're talking behind ___ you.
     C
They will never forget you till
D   G B7
Somebody new comes a-long.

Chorus 3

Em   A
Where you been late-ly?
Em   A
There's a new kid in town.
Em   A   Am7
Ev'rybody loves him, don't they?
      B7   E G♯m7
And he's holding her and you're still a-round.
     A B7
Oh, my, ___ my.

Outro

         E G♯m7 A
There's a new kid in town.
B7   E G♯m7 A Am
Just another new kid in town.
E   C♯m
(Oo, hoo.) Ev'rybody's talking 'bout the new kid in town.
E   C♯m
(Oo, hoo.) Ev'rybody's walking like the new kid in town.
E   C♯m
I don't want to hear it. I don't want to hear it.
 E C♯m E   C♯m
Ah, hoo.   Ev'rybody's talking.
       E C♯m E C♯m
People started walking. Mm. Mm.   ***Fade out***

No More Mr. Nice Guy

Words and Music by
Alice Cooper and Michael Bruce

Melody:

I used to be such a

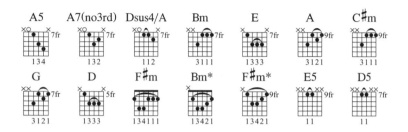

Intro

‖: A5 A7(no3rd) Dsus4/A │ N.C. :‖

│ Bm   │ E   │ Bm E   │

│ Bm   │ E   │   │

Verse 1

    A   C#m

I used to be such a sweet, sweet thing

           G   Bm D E

Till they   got a hold of me.

    A   C#m

I opened doors for little ___ old ladies,

G   Bm   D E

I helped the blind to see.

Pre-Chorus 1

    F#m   Bm*   D
I got no friends 'cause they read the papers.

                           E   F#m
They can't be seen with me.

                    Bm*   D   E   D
And I'm gettin' real shot down and I'm feelin' mean.

Chorus 1

F#m*   E5   D5
No more Mr. Nice Guy.

F#m*   N.C.
No more Mr. Clean.

F#m*   E5
No more Mr. Nice Guy.

         D5   F#m*   N.C.
They ____ say, "He's sick, he's ob-scene."

Interlude 1

A5 A7(no3rd) Dsus4/A N.C. A5 A7(no3rd) Dsus4/A N.C.
(Ooh.)

‖: A5 A7(no3rd) Dsus4/A │ N.C.   :‖

Pre-Chorus 2

F#m   Bm*   D
I got no friends 'cause they read the papers.

                           E   F#m
They can't be seen with me.

                    Bm*   D   E   D
And I'm feelin' real shot down and I'm, I'm gettin' mean.

Chorus 2   *Repeat Chorus 1*

Verse 2

  A   C#m
   My dog bit me on the leg today.

  G   Bm   E
   My cat clawed my eyes.

  A   C#m
   My mom's been thrown out of the social circle

  G   Bm   E A
   And dad has to hide.

              C#m
  I went to church incognito.

  G   Bm   D E A
  When ev'rybody rose

                 C#m
  The Rev'rend Smith he, he recognized me

  G   Bm
  And punched me in the nose.

  D E
  He said...

Chorus 3

    F#m*   E5   D5
‖: "No more Mr. Nice Guy.

F#m*   N.C.
No more Mr. Clean.

F#m*   E5
No more Mr. Nice Guy."

    D5   F#m*   N.C.
  He ___ said, "You're sick, you're ob-scene." :‖ *Repeat and fade*

The Pusher

Words and Music
by Hoyt Axton

Melody:

You know I smoked a lot of grass,

(Capo 3rd fret)

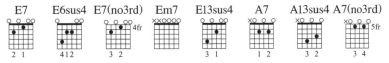

E7   E6sus4   E7(no3rd)   Em7   E13sus4   A7   A13sus4   A7(no3rd)

Intro   ‖: E7   E6sus4   E7(no3rd) │   E6sus4   Em7 │
│ E7   E6sus4   E7(no3rd) │   E13sus4   Em7 :‖   *Play 3 times*

Verse 1

         E7   E6sus4   E7(no3rd)
You know I smoked a lot of grass,

     E6sus4   Em7 E7 E6sus4 E7(no3rd) E13sus4 Em7
Oh, Lord, I popped a lot of pills.

E7   E6sus4   E7(no3rd)   E6sus4
  But I've never touched nothin',

   Em7 E7   E6sus4   E7(no3rd) E13sus4   Em7
Mm, hmm, that my spirit could kill.

A7   A13sus4   A7(no3rd)
  You know I've seen a lot of people walkin' round

     A13sus4   A7 A13sus4 A7(no3rd)   A13sus4   Em7
With tomb-stones in their eyes.

E7 E6sus4   E7(no3rd)   E6sus4
  But the pusher don't care,

Em7 E7   E7(no3rd)   E13sus4   Em7
Aw,   if you live or if you die.

	E7 E6sus4 E7(no3rd) E6sus4
Chorus 1	God damn,

                  Em7   E7   **E6sus4   E7(no3rd)   E13sus4   Em7**
Mm, hmm, the   pusher.

E7   E6sus4   E7(no3rd)
  God damn,

E6sus4   **Em7   E7   E6sus4   E7(no3rd)   E13sus4   Em7**
Yeah, hey, I say the push - er.

E7   E6sus4   E7(no3rd)
  I said, God damn,

            E6sus4   Em7   E7   E13sus4   E7
God damn   the pusher man.

Interlude 1	| **E7 E6sus4 E7(no3rd)** | **E6sus4 Em7** |
	| **E7 E6sus4 E7(no3rd)** | **E13sus4 Em7** |

	E7 E6sus4 E7(no3rd)
Verse 2	You know the dealer, the dealer is a man

E6sus4   **Em7   E7 E6sus4   E7(no3rd)   E13sus4   Em7**
With the love grass in his hand.

E7   E6sus4   **E7(no3rd)   E6sus4**
  But the pusher is a mon-ster,

            Em7   E7   E6sus4   E7(no3rd)   E13sus4   Em7
Good God, he's not a natural man.

A7   **A13sus4**   **A7(no3rd)**
  The deal-er for a nickel, Lord,

          A13sus4   **A7 A13sus4 A7(no3rd) A13sus4 Em7**
He'll sell you lots of sweet dreams.

E7 E6sus4   **E7(no3rd)   E6sus4**
  But the pusher'll ruin your body.

   Em7 E7   **E7(no3rd)**   **E13sus4   Em7**
Lord, he'll leave your, he'll leave your mind to scream.

| **Chorus 2** | *Repeat Chorus 1* |

| **Interlude 2** | *Repeat Interlude 1* |

Guitar Solo | N.C. |
            | E7   E6sus4   E7(no3rd) | E6sus4   Em7 |
            | E7   E6sus4   E7(no3rd) | E13sus4   Em7 |
            ‖:E7   E13sus4   E7(no3rd) | E13sus4   :‖ ***Play 6 times***

Verse 3

                  E7   E6sus4   E7(no3rd)
Well, now, if   I were the president

        E6sus4   Em7
Of this land, you know I'd declare

E7   E13sus4   E7(no3rd)   E13sus4
  Total war   on the pusher man.

E7   E6sus4
  I'd cut him if he stands and I'd

E7(no3rd)   E6sus4
  Shoot him if he'd run,

     E7   E13sus4   E7(no3rd)
And I'd kill him with my Bible

     E13sus4
And my razor and my gun.

Chorus 3   *Repeat Chorus 1*

Interlude 3   *Repeat Interlude 1*

Outro   ‖:E7   E6sus4   E7(no3rd) | E13sus4   :‖ ***Play 3 times***
          | E7

Owner of a Lonely Heart

Words and Music by Trevor Horn, Jon Anderson,
Trevor Rabin and Chris Squire

Melody:

Move your-self,

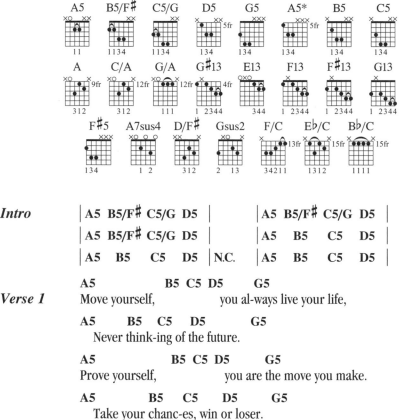

Intro

| A5 B5/F♯ C5/G D5 | | A5 B5/F♯ C5/G D5 | G5 A5* |

| A5 B5/F♯ C5/G D5 | | A5 B5 C5 D5 | G5 |

| A5 B5 C5 D5 | N.C. | A5 B5 C5 D5 | G5 |

Verse 1

    A5   B5 C5 D5   G5
Move yourself,   you al-ways live your life,

    A5   B5 C5 D5   G5
  Never think-ing of the future.

    A5   B5 C5 D5   G5
Prove yourself,   you are the move you make.

    A5   B5   C5   D5   G5
  Take your chanc-es, win or loser.

    A5   B5 C5 D5   G5
See yourself,   you are the steps you take.

    A5   B5   C5   D5   G5
  You and you, and that's the only way.

    A5   B5 C5   D5   G5
Shake,   shake your-self, you're ev-'ry move you make,

    A5   B5 C5 D5 G5
So the sto   -   ry goes.

Chorus 1

A5   B5 C5 D5   G5
Owner of a   lone-ly heart.

A5   B5 C5 D5
Owner of a   lone-ly heart.

         G5
(Oo, much ___ better than a)

A5   B5 C5 D5   G5
Owner of a   bro-ken heart.

A5   B5 C5 D5
Owner of a   lone-ly heart.

Verse 2

A5 B5 C5   D5   G5
   Say you don't want to chance it,

A5   B5 C5   D5   G5
   You've been hurt so ___ before.

A5   B5 C5 D5   G5
Watch it, now,   the ea-gle in the sky,

A5   B5   C5   D5
   How he danc-in' one and only.

A5 B5 C5   D5   G5
You   lose your-self, no, not for pity's sake.

A5   B5 C5   D5
   There's no real reason to be lonely.

A5   B5 C5 D5   G5
Be yourself,   give your freewill a chance.

A5   B5 C5 D5   G5
   You've got to   want to succeed.

Chorus 2

```
A5        B5  C5  D5        G5
Owner of a     lone-ly heart.

A5        B5  C5  D5
Owner of a     lone-ly heart.

          G5
(Oo, much ___ better than a)

A5        B5  C5  D5        G5
Owner of a     bro-ken heart.

A5        B5  C5     D5 A
Owner of a     lonely ___ heart.
```

Bridge 1

```
|A           |C/A  G/A  |A            |

       C/A    G/A    A  C/A  G/A
Own - er of a lonely heart.

          A                  C/A
After my own indecision they con-fused me so.

G/A            A                    C/A G/A
  My love said, "Never question your will at all."

        A                  C/A          G/A
In the end you've got to go, look before you leap,

A                       G♯13
And don't you hesitate at all, no, no.  Yow!

E13 F13  F♯13  G13 G♯13 A5
Ah, ah,   ah,   ah, ah,  yow!
```

Guitar Solo

```
|A5  B5  C5  D5  |   G5    |A5  B5  C5  D5  |   G5           |
|A5  B5  C5  D5  |         |A5  B5  C5  D5  |   G5  F♯5 G5   |
||:A5  B5  C5  D5  |   G5    |A5  B5  C5  D5  |   G5          :||
```

Interlude

```
||:A7sus4  D/F♯ |   Gsus2   :|| Play 4 times
```

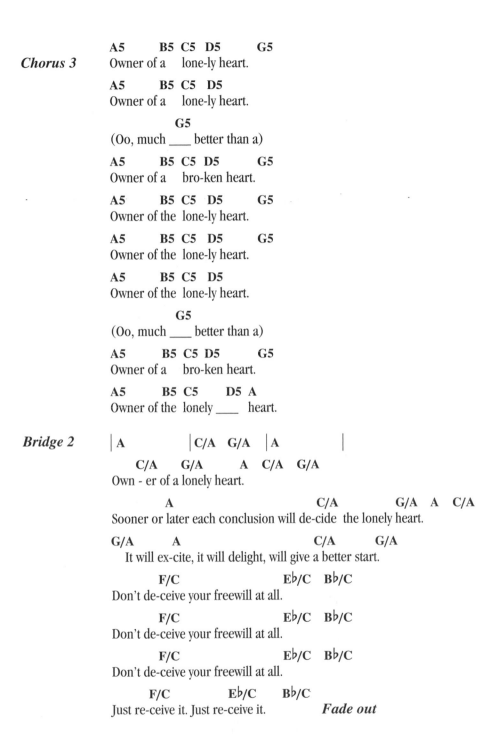

Chorus 3

A5   B5 C5 D5   G5
Owner of a   lone-ly heart.

A5   B5 C5 D5
Owner of a   lone-ly heart.

             G5
(Oo, much ___ better than a)

A5   B5 C5 D5   G5
Owner of a   bro-ken heart.

A5   B5 C5 D5   G5
Owner of the lone-ly heart.

A5   B5 C5 D5   G5
Owner of the lone-ly heart.

A5   B5 C5 D5
Owner of the lone-ly heart.

             G5
(Oo, much ___ better than a)

A5   B5 C5 D5   G5
Owner of a   bro-ken heart.

A5   B5 C5   D5 A
Owner of the lonely ___ heart.

Bridge 2

| A | C/A G/A | A |

    C/A   G/A   A C/A G/A
Own - er of a lonely heart.

             A   C/A   G/A A C/A
Sooner or later each conclusion will de-cide the lonely heart.

G/A   A   C/A   G/A
   It will ex-cite, it will delight, will give a better start.

       F/C   E♭/C B♭/C
Don't de-ceive your freewill at all.

       F/C   E♭/C B♭/C
Don't de-ceive your freewill at all.

       F/C   E♭/C B♭/C
Don't de-ceive your freewill at all.

       F/C   E♭/C B♭/C
Just re-ceive it. Just re-ceive it.   *Fade out*

Paranoid

Words and Music by Anthony Iommi,
John Osbourne, William Ward and
Terence Butler

Fin-ished with _ my wom - an 'cause _ she

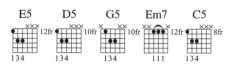

E5   D5   G5   Em7   C5

Intro

‖: E5 | N.C.   :‖ *Play 4 times*

Verse 1

E5
Finished with my woman

               D5   G5 D5 E5   Em7
'Cause she couldn't help me with my mind.

E5
People think I'm insane

          D5   G5 D5 E5
Because I ____ am frowning all   the time.

Interlude 1

‖: E5   C5 | D5 | E5 | :‖

Verse 2

E5
All day long I think of things,

       D5   G5 D5 E5   Em7
But nothing seems to sat - is - fy.

E5
Think I'll lose my mind if I don't

      D5   G5 D5 E5
Find ____ something to pass it   by.

Bridge

E5   D5
Can you help me?

                       E5
Thought you were my friend.

       D5
Whoa, yeah!

| *Interlude 2* | ‖: E5 | | D5 | G5 D5 E5 Em7 :‖ |

                              E5

Verse 3   I need someone to show me

                          D5   G5 D5 E5   Em7

The things ____ in life that I   can't find.

E5   D5

I can't see the things that make true hap - piness,

  G5   D5 E5

  I must be   blind.

| *Guitar Solo* | ‖: E5 | | D5 | G5 D5 E5 Em7 :‖ *Play 4 times* |

Interlude 3   *Repeat Interlude 2*

                              E5

Verse 4   Make a joke and I will sigh

                          D5   G5 D5 E5   Em7

And you ____ will laugh and I   will cry.

E5

Happiness I cannot feel

                          D5   G5 D5 E5

And love ____ to me is so   un - real.

Interlude 4   *Repeat Interlude 1*

                              E5

Verse 5   And so as you hear these words

                          D5   G5 D5 E5   Em7

Telling ____ you now of ____ my state.

E5

I tell you to enjoy life,

                          D5   G5 D5 E5

I wish ____ I could but it's   too late.

| *Outro* | \| E5   \| \| D5   \| G5 D5 E5 Em7 \| |
| | \| E5   \| \| D5   \| G5 D5 E5   \| |

The Passenger

Words and Music by
Iggy Pop and Ricky Gardner

Melody:

I am the pas-sen - ger, ____

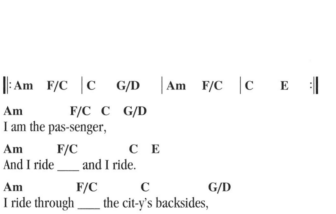

Am   F/C   C   G/D   E

Intro   ‖: Am F/C │C G/D │Am F/C │C   E   :‖

                    Am   **F/C C G/D**
Verse 1   I am the pas-senger,

                    Am   **F/C**   **C   E**
                    And I ride ____ and I ride.

                    Am   **F/C**   **C**   **G/D**
                    I ride through ____ the cit-y's backsides,

                    Am   **F/C**   **C**   **E**
                    I see the stars ____ come out of the sky.

                    Am   **F/C**   **C**   **G/D**
                      Yeah, the bright ____ and hol-low sky,

                    Am   **F/C**   **C**   **E**
                    You know it looks ____ so good ____ tonight.

Interlude 1   │Am F/C │C G/D │Am F/C │C   E   │

Verse 2

Am   F/C C G/D
I am the pas-senger,

Am   F/C   C   E
I stay un - der glass.

Am   F/C   C   G/D
I look through ____ my win-dow so bright,

Am   F/C   C   E
I see the stars ____ come out ____ tonight.

Am   F/C   C   G/D
I see the bright ____ and hol-low sky

Am   F/C   C   E
Over the cit-y's ripped backside.

Am   F/C   C   G/D Am F/C C E
And ev'rything looks good ____ tonight.

Chorus 1

          Am   F/C   C   G/D
Singing, la, ____ la, la, ____ la, la, la, la, la.

    Am   F/C   C   E
La, ____ la, la, ____ la, la, la, la, la.

    Am   F/C   C   G/D Am   F/C
La, ____ la, la, ____ la, la, la, la, la, la, la, la.
| C   E |Am F/C |C   G/D |

Verse 3

Am   F/C C G/D
Get into the car,

Am   F/C   C E
We'll be the ____ passenger.

Am   F/C   C   G/D
We'll ride through ____ the cit-y tonight,

Am   F/C   C   E
We'll see the cit-y's ripped ____ backsides.

Am   F/C   C   G/D
We'll see the bright ____ and hol-low sky,

Am   F/C   C   E
We'll see the stars ____ that shine ____ so bright.

Am   F/C C   G/D Am F/C C E
Stars made for us ____ tonight.

| *Interlude 2* | *Repeat Interlude 1* |

| | Am   F/C C   G/D |
| *Verse 4* | Oh, the pas-senger, |

Am   F/C   C   E
  How, how he rides.

Am   F/C C   G/D
  Oh, the pas-senger,

Am   F/C   C   E
And he rides and he rides.

Am   F/C   C   G/D
He looks through his win-dow.

Am   F/C C   E
  What does he see?

Am   F/C   C   G/D
He sees the sign ___ and hol - low sky,

Am   F/C   C   E
He sees the stars ___ come out ___ tonight.

| | Am   F/C   C   G/D |
| *Verse 5* | He sees the cit-y's ripped backsides, |

Am   F/C   C   E
He sees the wind - ing o-cean drive.

Am   F/C   C   G/D
And ev'rything was made for you and me,

Am   F/C   C   E
  All of it was made for you and me,

Am   F/C   C   G/D
'Cause it just ___belongs ___ to you and me,

Am   F/C   C   E
So let's take a ride and see what's mine.

Interlude 3   *Repeat Interlude 1*

Chorus 2   *Repeat Chorus 1*

Verse 6

     Am   F/C C   G/D
Oh, the pas-senger,

     Am   F/C   C   E
  He rides and he rides.

     Am   F/C   C   G/D
He sees things ___ from un-der glass,

     Am   F/C   C   E
He looks through his win-dow inside.

     Am   F/C   C   G/D
He sees the things that he knows ___ are his,

     Am   F/C C   E
He sees the bright and hol-low sky.

     Am   F/C   C   G/D
He sees the cit-y sleep at night,

     Am   F/C   C   E
He sees the stars ___ are out tonight.

     Am   F/C   C   G/D
And all of it is yours ___ and mine,

     Am   F/C   C   E
And all of it is yours ___ and mine.

     Am   F/C   C
So let's ride, ___ and ride,

          G/D   Am F/C C E Am F/C C
And ride, ___ and ride.

Chorus 3

    G/D   Am   F/C   C   G/D
‖: Ah, singing, la, ___la, la, ___ la, la, la, la, la.

      Am   F/C   C   E
La, ___ la, la, ___ la, la, la, la, la.

      Am   F/C   C   G/D Am F/C C
La, ___ la, la, ___ la, la, la, la, la, la, la, la.   :‖ *Repeat and fade*

Radar Love

Words and Music by
George Kooymans and Barry Hay

I been driv - in' all night, _ my hand's

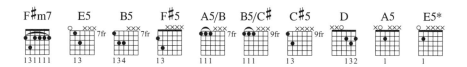

F#m7   E5   B5   F#5   A5/B   B5/C#   C#5   D   A5   E5*

Intro   ‖: F#m7 | :‖ *Play 24 times*

                                F#m7

Verse 1   I been driv - in' all night, my hand's wet on the wheel.

                 There's a voice in my head that drives my heel.

                 It's my baby callin', says, "I need you here."

                 And it's a half past four and I'm shiftin' gear.

                 E5   **B5**   **F#5**

Pre-Chorus 1   When she is lonely and the long - ing gets too much,

                 E5   **B5**   **A5/B** **B5/C#**

                 She sends a cable coming in ___ from above.

                 C#5   **B5/C#**

                 Don't need a phone at all.

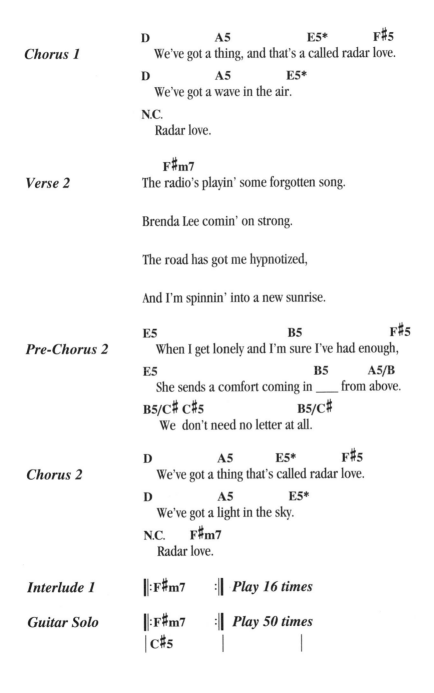

Chorus 1

    D   A5   E5*   F#5
    We've got a thing, and that's a called radar love.

    D   A5   E5*
    We've got a wave in the air.

    N.C.
    Radar love.

Verse 2

      F#m7
    The radio's playin' some forgotten song.

    Brenda Lee comin' on strong.

    The road has got me hypnotized,

    And I'm spinnin' into a new sunrise.

Pre-Chorus 2

    E5   B5   F#5
    When I get lonely and I'm sure I've had enough,

    E5   B5   A5/B
    She sends a comfort coming in ___ from above.

    B5/C# C#5   B5/C#
    We don't need no letter at all.

Chorus 2

    D   A5   E5*   F#5
    We've got a thing that's called radar love.

    D   A5   E5*
    We've got a light in the sky.

    N.C.   F#m7
    Radar love.

Interlude 1   ‖:F#m7   :‖ *Play 16 times*

Guitar Solo   ‖:F#m7   :‖ *Play 50 times*
                 |C#5 | |

Breakdown	‖: N.C. :‖ *Play 41 times*

Interlude 2	‖: F#m7 :‖ *Play 16 times*

Verse 3

F#m7
No more speed, I'm almost there.

Gotta keep cool, now, gotta take care.

Last car to pass, here I go!

And the line of cars drove down real slow, whoa.

And the radio played that forgotten song.

Brenda Lee, it's comin' on strong.

And the news man sang his same song.

Oh, one more radar lover gone.

Pre-Chorus 3

Repeat Pre-Chorus 2

Chorus 3

D   A5   E5*   F#5
We've got a thing that's called radar love.
D   A5   E5* F#5
We've got a light in the sky.
D   A5   E5*   F#5
We've got a thing that's called a radar love.
D   A5   E5*   N.C.   F#m7
   We've got a thing that's called   radar love.

Outro

‖: F#m7 :‖ *Play 16 times*

Renegade

Words and Music
by Tommy Shaw

Melody:

Oh, __ ma-ma, I'm in fear for my

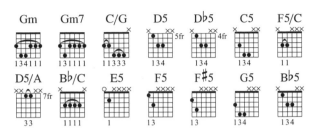

Gm   Gm7   C/G   D5   D♭5   C5   F5/C
D5/A   B♭/C   E5   F5   F♯5   G5   B♭5

Intro

N.C.(Gm)
Oh, mama, I'm in fear for my life from the long arm of the law.

Lawman has put an end to my running and I'm so far from my home.

Oh, mama, I can hear you a crying, you're so scared and all alone.

Hangman is coming down from the gallows and I don't have very long.

Chorus 1

            Gm7 C/G   Gm7   C/G
The jig is up, the news is out,

            Gm7   C/G   Gm7
They've finally ____ found me.

            C/G   Gm7 C/G
The rene-gade who had it made

    Gm7   C/G   Gm7
Re-trieved for a boun-ty.

D5   D♭5
    Never more to go astray,

C5
    This will be the end today

F5/C Gm7   C/G   Gm7   C/G   Gm7   C/G   D5/A
Of the want - ed man.

Verse

Gm7
Oh, mama, I've been years on the lam

   Bb/C   **Gm**
And had a high price on my head.

Gm7
Lawman said, "Get him dead or alive,"

   Bb/C   **Gm**
Now it's for sure he'll see me dead.

Gm7
Dear mama, I can hear you a crying,

   Bb/C   **Gm**
You're so ___ scared and all a-lone.

Gm7
Hangman is coming down from the gallows

    Bb/C   **Gm**
And I don't ___ have very long.

Chorus 2

  Gm7 C/G Gm7 C/G
The jig is up, the news is out,

    Gm7 C/G   Gm7
They've finally ___ found me.

    C/G   Gm7 C/G
The rene-gade who had it made

  Gm7   C/G   Gm7
Re-trieved for a boun-ty.

D5
  Never more to go astray,

Db5 C5
The   judge will have revenge today

F5/C Gm7 C/G   Gm7 C/G Gm7 C/G Gm7
On the want - ed man.

Interlude 1 | N.C. | **E5 F5 F#5** |

| Guitar Solo | ‖:Gm7 | | F5/C Gm7 :‖ *Play 7 times* |
| | Gm7 | G5 B♭5 C5 | |

| Interlude 2 | C5 | G5 B♭5 C5 | | G5 B♭5 D5 |
| | | B♭5 C5 D5 | |C5 B♭5 C5 B♭5 |

Interlude 3

G5 N.C.
Oh, mama, I'm in fear for my life from the long arm of the law.

Hangman is coming down from the gallows and I don't have very long.

Chorus 3

Gm7 C/G   Gm7   C/G
The jig is   up, the news is out,

   Gm7   C/G   Gm7
They've finally ___ found me.

    C/G   Gm7   C/G
The rene-gade who had it made

  Gm7   C/G   Gm7
Re-trieved for a boun-ty.

D5   D♭5
  Never more to go astray,

C5
  This will be the end today

    Gm7 C/G Gm7 C/G Gm7 C/G
Of the want - ed man,

   Gm7   F5/C Gm7   F5/C Gm7
The wanted man.

      F5/C Gm7   F5/C Gm7
And I don't wanna go,   oh, no.

| Outro | ‖:Gm7 | | F5/C Gm7 :‖ *Repeat and fade* |

Ramblin' Man

Words and Music
by Dickey Betts

Tune up 1/2 step:
(low to high) E#–A#–D#–G#–B#–E#

Lord, I __ was born __ a ram - blin'

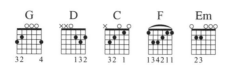

G   D   C   F   Em

Intro |G |D |C | G |

Chorus 1

G		F	C	G

Lord, I was born ____ a ram - blin' man.

                          C   D
Try'n' to make a living, and doin' the best I ____ can.

     C   G   Em   C
An' when it's time for leavin' I hope you'll understand,

G   D   G
That I was born ____ a ramblin' man.

Verse 1

           G   C   G
Well, my father was a gam - bler down in Georgia,

                        C   D
And he wound up on the wrong ____ end of a gun.

     C   G   Em   C
And I was born in the back seat of a Greyhound bus,

G   D   G
Rollin' down Highway 41.

Chorus 2   *Repeat Chorus 1*

Interlude 1 | D N.C. | | | |

Guitar Solo 1
G	C	G		
	C	D		
C	G	Em	C	
G	D	G		

Verse 2

         G   C   G
I'm on my way to New ____ Orleans this mornin',

                  C   D
And leavin' out of Nashville, Tennessee.

          C   G   Em   C
They're always havin' a good ____ time down on the bayou, Lord.

         G   D   G
Them delta women think the world of me.

Chorus 3   *Repeat Chorus 1*

Chorus 4

         G   F   C   G
‖: Lord, I was born ____ a ram - blin' man. :‖ *Play 4 times*

Interlude 2   ‖: G |F   C |G | :‖

Guitar Solo 2 ‖: G |F   C |G | :‖ *Repeat and fade*

Rhiannon

Words and Music
by Stevie Nicks

Melody:

Rhi - an-non   rings ____ like a

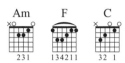

Am   F   C

231   134211   32 1

Intro   ‖: Am | |F | :‖

Verse 1

          Am
          Rhi-annon rings like a bell through the night.

          F
          And wouldn't you love to love her?

Am
          Takes to the sky like a bird in flight.

          F
          And who will be her lover?

Pre-Chorus 1

          C   **F**
          All your life you've never seen a woman ____ taken by the wind.

          C
          Would you stay if she promised you heaven?

          F
          Will you ever win?

	Am
Verse 2	She is like a cat in the dark.

       F
And then she is the darkness.

Am
   She rules her life like a flying skylark.

         F
And when ____ the sky is starlets.

       C   **F**

Pre-Chorus 2 All your life you've never seen a woman ____ taken by the wind.

C
   Would you stay if she promised you heaven?

F
   Will you ever win? Will you ever win?

       Am   **F** **Am**

Chorus 1   Rhi-an-non.

          F **Am**
Rhi-an-non.

          F **Am**
Rhi-an-non.

          F   **N.C.**
Rhi-annon.

	Am
Verse 3	She rings like a bell through the night.

F

And wouldn't you love to love her?

Am

She rules her life like a bird in flight.

F

And who will be her lover?

Pre-Chorus 3   *Repeat Pre-Chorus 2*

	Am F Am
Chorus 2	Rhi-an-non.

F   Am

Rhi-an-non.

F   Am

Rhi-an-non.

F   **Am**

Tak - en by, taken by the sky.

F   **Am**

Taken by, taken by the sky.

F   **Am   F**

Tak - en by, taken by the sky.

Guitar Solo   ‖: Am | | F | :‖ *Play 4 times*

	Am **F**
Outro	Dreams unwind, love's a state of mind.

Am   **F   Am**

Dreams unwind, love's a state of mind.   *Fade out*

Rock and Roll All Nite

Words and Music by
Paul Stanley and Gene Simmons

Tune down 1/2 step:
(low to high) E♭–A♭–D♭–G♭–B♭–E♭

Melody:

You show us ev - 'ry - thing you've got. __

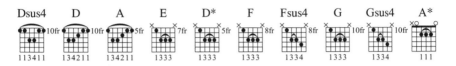

Dsus4 D A E D* F Fsus4 G Gsus4 A*

Intro | Dsus4 | D Dsus4 D A | E | A |

| | E | A | |

Verse 1

      A   E   A
You show us ev-'rything you've got.

      E   D*
You keep on dancing and the room gets hot.

      E   Dsus4 D Dsus4 D A
You drive us wild; we'll drive you cra-zy.

      E   A
And you say you wan-na go for a spin.

      E   D*
The party's just begun; we'll let you in.

      E   Dsus4 D Dsus4 D E F
You drive us wild; we'll drive you cra-zy.

Pre-Chorus 1

      Fsus4 F   G Gsus4 G   Gsus4 G N.C.
You keep on shoutin', you keep on shout-in'.

Come on!

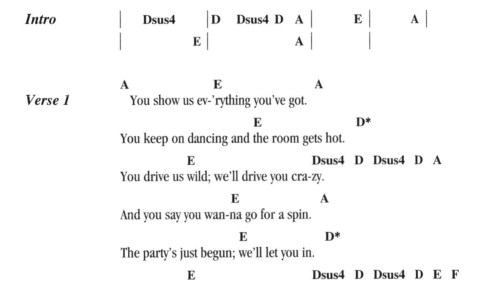

Chorus 1

A*   **D**
I wanna rock and roll all night,

E
   And party every day.

A*   **D**
I wanna rock and roll all night,

E
   And party every day.

A*   **N.C.**
I wanna rock and roll all night,

And party every day.

I wanna rock and roll all night,

And party every day.

Interlude 1 | **Dsus4** | **D**   **Dsus4 D   A** |

Verse 2

                        E   **A**
You keep on sayin' you'll be mine for a while.

                      E   **D***
You're looking fancy and I like your style.

                 E   **Dsus4 D Dsus4 D A**
And you drive us wild; we'll drive you cra-zy.

                 E   **A**
And you show us ev-'rything you've got.

               E   **D***
Oh, baby, baby, that's quite a lot.

                 E   **Dsus4 D Dsus4 D E F**
And you drive us wild; we'll drive you cra-zy.

Pre-Chorus 2

   Fsus4   **F**   **G   Gsus4 G**   **Gsus4 G**   **N.C.**
You keep on shoutin', you keep   on shout-in'.

I can't hear ya!

Chorus 2	*Repeat Chorus 1*		
Interlude 2	*Repeat Interlude 1*		

Guitar Solo

```
|A*    E  |     A* |     E  |                 D  |
|      E  |        | Dsus4  |D Dsus4 D Dsus4  A* |
|      E  |     A* |     E  |                 D  |
|      E  |        | Dsus4  |D Dsus4 D        F  |
```

Interlude 3

Fsus4   F   G   Gsus4 G   Gsus4 G N.C.
You keep on shoutin'. You keep   on shout-in'.   What?

Chorus 3

A*   D
I wanna rock and roll all night,

E
   And party every day.

A*   D
I wanna rock and roll all night,

E
   And party every day.

A*   N.C.
I wanna rock and roll all night,

And party every day.

A*   N.C.
I wanna rock and roll all night,

And party every day.

Outro

```
|  Dsus4         |D   Dsus4 D  F |   Fsus4  F  G |
|  Gsus4  G  Gsus4 |N.C.          |          A*   |
|               |               |               |
```

Ridin' the Storm Out

Words and Music
by Gary Richrath

Melody:

Rid - in' the storm _ out,

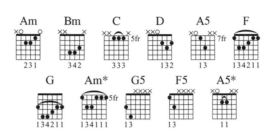

Am   Bm   C   D   A5   F

G   Am*   G5   F5   A5*

Intro   ‖: Am   Bm   C | Bm   Am :‖   *Play 4 times*

Verse 1

        Bm   C   Bm Am
Ridin' ____ the storm out,

           Bm   C   Bm
Waitin' for ____ the thaw out

      Am
On a full moon night

Bm C   Bm   Am   Bm C Bm Am
In the Rocky Mountain winter.

          Bm C   Bm
Wine bot-tle's low

Am   Bm C   Bm
Watchin' for the   snow

                Bm C   Bm   Am
And thinkin' about what I've been missin' in the city.

Pre-Chorus 1

         D   **A5**
And I'm ___ not missin' a thing,

D   **Am**
Watchin' the full moon crossing the range.

Chorus 1

F   **G**   **Am***   **G5 F5**
  Rid-in' the storm out.

F   **G**   **Am***   **G5 F5**
Rid-in' the storm out.

F   **G**   **Am***   **G5 F5**
Rid-in' the storm out.

F   **G**   **Am***   **Bm C**
Rid-in' the storm out.

| **Bm Am** | **Bm C** | **Bm Am** |

Verse 2

       Bm   **C**   **Bm Am**
Lady ___ be-side me,

            Bm   **C**   **Bm Am**
Well, she's there ___ to guide me.

        Bm   **C**
She says a that a - lone,

       Bm   **Am**   **Bm C Bm**
We've a finally found our home.

        Am   **Bm C**   **Bm**
Well, the wind outside is a   fright'nin',

       Am   **Bm C**   **Bm**
But it's kinder than a light-nin' life in the city.

      Bm C   **Bm**   **Am**
A hard life to   live, but it gives back a what you give.

Pre-Chorus 2   *Repeat Pre-Chorus 1*

Chorus 2

F   G   Am*   G5 F5
   Rid-in' the storm out.

F G   Am*   G5 F5
Rid-in' the storm out.

   G Am*   G5 F5
Rid-in' the storm out.

     G   Am*   G5 Am
Rid-in' the storm out.

      G   Am* G Am* G
Whoa, ____ yes, I ____ am.

Guitar Solo 1

A5*	N.C.		A5*	N.C.	
G	F	G	Am*	G F	
	G	Am* G F		G	
Am G F		G		A5*	
	Bm C	Bm Am		Bm C	
	Bm Am				

Verse 3

      Bm   C   Bm
Ridin' ____ the storm out,

     Am   Bm C Bm
I'm a waitin' for the   thaw ____ out

     Am
On a full moon night

Bm   C   Bm   Am   Bm C   Bm Am
In the Rocky Mountain kind a winter. Oh, yeah.

      Bm C   Bm
Wine bot-tle's low

     Am   Bm C   Bm
I'm a watchin' for the   snow.

Am   Bm C   Bm   Am
I'm thinkin' about what I've been a missin' in the city.

Pre-Chorus 3

N.C.   D   A5

Oh, ho, ho, well, I'm ____ not missin' a thing,

         D   Am

I'm a watchin' the full moon crossin' the range.

Chorus 3

F   G   Am*   G5   F5

Rid-in' the storm out.

F   G   Am*   G5   F5

Rid-in' the storm out.

F   G   Am*   G5   F5

Rid-in' the storm out.

F   G   F5

  Rid - in',

F   G   F5

  Rid - in',

F   G   A5

  Rid - in' the storm out.

Oh, no. Oh, no. Oh, oh, oh, oh, oh.

Guitar Solo 2 ‖:Am   Bm C | Bm Am :‖ *Play 16 times*

Outro | F | G | | |

| | |Am | |

| | | | |

Lord, ya' know I'm ridin'.

Lord, ya' know I'm ride.

Lord, ya' know I'm ridin' the storm out. Hey, uh.

Run to You

Words and Music by
Bryan Adams and Jim Vallance

Melody:

She   says her love for me

(Capo 2nd fret)

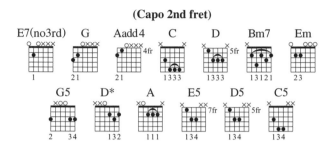

E7(no3rd) G Aadd4 C D Bm7 Em

G5 D* A E5 D5 C5

Intro   ‖: **E7(no3rd)** |**G**   **Aadd4** :‖ *Play 4 times*

         E7(no3rd)   G   Aadd4

Verse 1   She says her love for me

                 E7(no3rd)   G Aadd4
         Could never die.

         E7(no3rd)   G   Aadd4
         But that'd change if she ever found ____ out

                 E7(no3rd)   G Aadd4
         About you and I.

         E7(no3rd)   G   Aadd4
          Oh, but her love is cold.

         E7(no3rd)   G   Aadd4
         Wouldn't hurt her if she didn't know, 'cause...

         C
          When it gets too much,

         D   Bm7
          I need to feel your touch.

Chorus 1

              Em   **G5** **D*** **A**

I'm gonna run to you.

              Em   **G5** **D*** **A**

I'm gonna run to you.

                   Em   **G5**

'Cause when the feelin's right

            D*   **A**

I'm gon-na run all night,

              Em   **G5**

I'm gonna run to you.

Interlude 1   ‖: **E7(no3rd)**   │**G**   **Aadd4** :‖

Verse 2

E7(no3rd) **G**   **Aadd4**

  She's got a heart of gold,

            E7(no3rd)   **G** **Aadd4**

She'd never let me down.

E7(no3rd)   **G**   **Aadd4**

  But you're the one that always turns me on,

          E7(no3rd)   **G** **Aadd4**

You keep me comin' 'round.

E7(no3rd) **G**   **Aadd4**

  I know her love is true,

          E7(no3rd)   **G**   **Aadd4**

But it's so damn easy makin' love to you.

C

  I got my mind made up,

D   **Bm7**

  I need to feel your touch.

	Em **G5** **D*** **A**

Chorus 2   **Em**   **G5** **D*** **A**

                      I'm gonna run to you.

                             Em   **G5** **D*** **A**

Yeah, I'm gonna run to you.

                           Em   **G5**

'Cause when the feelin's right

               D*   **A**

I'm gon-na stay all night,

                    Em   **G5** **D***

I'm gonna run to you.

                           Em   **G5** **D***

Yeah, I'm gonna run to you.

A   **Em**   **G5**

Oh, when the feelin's right

         D*   **A**

I'm gon-na run all night,

                  Em   **G5** **D***

I'm gonna run to you.

Interlude 2 | **E5** | | **D5** | |

                                  When the feelin's right, now.

              | **C5** | | **D5** | |

                                        Oh.

              | **E5** | | **D5** | |

              | **C5** | | **D5** | |

              | **Em** **G5** **D***| **A** | **Em** **G5** **D***| **A** |

                                        Oh,   I'm gonna

```
                    Em       G5  D*  A
Chorus 3            Run to you.

                              Em       G5  D*  A
                    Yeah, I'm gonna run to you.

                              Em      G5
                    'Cause when the feelin's right

                        D*         A
                    I'm gon-na stay all night,

                              Em       G5  D*
                    I'm gonna run to you.

                    A            Em       G5  D*
                    Oh,  I'm gonna run to you.

                    A                Em      G5
                    Yeah, and when the feelin's right

                        D*        A       Em
                    I'm gon-na stay all night.

                    G5        D*        A
                    Oh, when the feelin's right, now.
```

Outro   ‖:Em G5 D*│   A   │Em G5 D*│   A   :‖ *Repeat and fade*
                                                (w/voc. ad lib.)

Since You've Been Gone

Words and Music
by Russell Ballard

Melody:

I get the same _ old dreams,

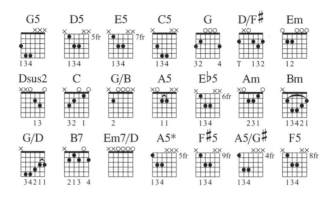

Intro

| G5 D5 | E5 C5 | G5 D5 E5 | C5 D5 |
| G5 D5 | E5 C5 | G5 D5 E5 | C5 | D5 | |

                 Whoa.

Verse 1

G   D/F#
 I get the same ____ old dreams,

Em   Dsus2
 Same time ev'ry night.

C   G/B   A5 Dsus2
 Fall to the ground and I wake up.

G   D/F#
 So I get outta bed,

    Em   Dsus2
Put on ____ my shoes and in ____ my head

C   G/B   A5 Dsus2
 Thoughts slide back to the break up.

Pre-Chorus 1

Eb5   N.C.(F)
These four walls are closin' in.

Eb5   N.C.
Look at the fix you put me in.

Chorus 1

G5   D5
Since you been gone,

E5   C5
Since you been gone,

  G5   D5 E5 C5 D5
I'm outta my head, can't take it.

G5   D5
Could I be wrong?

  E5   C5
But since you been gone

G5   D5 E5   C5 D5
You cast a spell, so   break it.

G5 D5 E5   C5 G5 D5
Ohh.   Whoa.   Whoa.

E5 C5   D5
        Since you been gone.

Verse 2

G   D/F#
  So, in the night ____ I stand

Em   Dsus2
  Beneath the back ___ street light.

C   G/B   A5   Dsus2
  I read the words ___ that you sent to me.

G   D/F#
  I can take the afternoon,

  Em   Dsus2
The nighttime comes a-round too soon.

C   G/B   A5   Dsus2
  You can't know what you mean to me.

Pre-Chorus 2

Eb5   N.C.(F)
  Your poison letter, your telegram,

Eb5   N.C.
  Just goes to show you don't give a damn.

Chorus 2   *Repeat Chorus 1*

Guitar Solo 1 | G Am | Bm C | G/D B7 | Em Em7/D |
                          | C A5 Dsus2 |

Interlude

                  G   Am   Bm C
                  If you will come back, baby,

                    G/D   B7   Em Em7/D C A5 Dsus2 D5
                  You know you'll never do wrong.

Chorus 3

                  A5*   E5
                  Since you been gone,

                  F#5   D5
                  Since you been gone,

                   A5*   E5 F#5 D5 E5
                  I'm outta my head, can't take it.

                  A5*   E5
                  Could I be wrong?

                   F#5   D5
                  But since you been gone

                  A5*   E5 F#5 D5 E5
                  You cast a spell, so   break it.

                  A5* A5/G# F#5 F5 E5   F#5   F5
                  Whoa.   Whoa.   Whoa. Whoa.

                  E5   A5*
                  Ever since you been gone.

Guitar Solo 2 ||: A5* E5 | F#5 D5 | A5* E5 F#5 | D5   E5   :||

Outro

                   A5*   E5
                  ||: Since you been gone,

                  F#5   D5
                  Since you been gone,

                   A5*   E5 F#5 D5 E5
                  I'm outta my head, can't take it.   :|| *Repeat and fade*

Smoke on the Water

Words and Music by Ritchie Blackmore,
Ian Gillan, Roger Glover, Jon Lord and Ian Paice

Melody:

We   all   came   out   to Mon - treaux

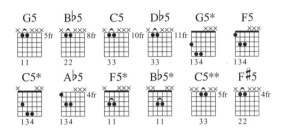

| G5 | Bb5 | C5 | Db5 | G5* | F5 |

| C5* | Ab5 | F5* | Bb5* | C5** | F#5 |

Intro

‖: G5 Bb5 C5 G5 | Bb5 Db5 C5 |

| G5 Bb5 C5 Bb5 | G5   :‖ ***Play 5 times***

| G5 Bb5 C5 G5 | Bb5 Db5 C5 |

| G5 Bb5 C5 Bb5 | G5   C5 |

                    G5*
Verse 1   We all came out to Montreaux

                              F5   **G5***
                 On the Lake Gene - va shore - line

                 To make records with the mobile,
                 F5   **G5***
                   We didn't have much time.

                 But Frank Zappa and the Mothers
                              F5   **G5***
                 Were at the best place around.

                 But some stupid with a flare gun
                              F5   **G5***
                 Burned the place to the ground.

Chorus 1

       C5*   **A♭5**   **G5***
Smoke on the water,   a fire in the sky.

C5*   **A♭5**
Smoke on the water.

Interlude 1

G5 B♭5 C5 G5	B♭5 D♭5 C5
G5 B♭5 C5 B♭5	G5
G5 B♭5 C5 B♭5	G5 D♭5 C5
G5 B♭5 C5 B♭5	G5 C5

Verse 2

G5*
   They burned down the gambling house,

                 F5   **G5***
It died in an awful sound.

A Funky Claude was running in and out,

F5   **G5***
   Pulling kids out the ground.

                                 F5   **G5***
When it all was over, we had to find an-other place.

But Swiss time was running out:

                 F5   **G5***
It seemed that we would lose the race.

Chorus 2   *Repeat Chorus 1*

Interlude 2   *Repeat Interlude 1*

Guitar Solo

	: G5*		C5*	G5*
		C5*	G5* :	
C5*		F5	

Interlude 3   *Repeat Interlude 1*

	G5*
Verse 3	We ended up at the Grand Hotel,

G5*
We ended up at the Grand Hotel,

    F5   **G5***
It was empty, cold and bare.

But with the Rolling truck Stones thing just outside,

F5   **G5***
  Making our music there.

With a few red lights, a few old beds,

      F5   **G5***
We made a place to sweat.

No matter what we get out of this,

     F5   **G5***
I know,   I know we'll never forget.

Chorus 3   *Repeat Chorus 1*

Interlude 4

‖: G5 Bb5 C5 G5 |Bb5 Db5 C5 |
|G5 Bb5 C5 Bb5 |G5   :‖ *Play 4 times*

Organ Solo

‖: F5* G5   Bb5* F5*   G5 :‖
‖: Bb5* G5 F5* G5 F5* G5 :‖ *Play 3 times*
|Bb5* C5** F5* G5 F5* G5 |
|Bb5* G5 F5* G5 | F5* F#5 |
|G5 | |
|Bb5* G5 F5* G5 | | *Fade out*

Smokin' in the Boys Room

Words and Music by
Michael Koda and Michael Lutz

Tune down 1 step:
(low to high) D–G–C–F–A–D

Melody:

I'm sit - tin' in the class - room,

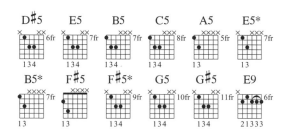

D#5   E5   B5   C5   A5   E5*

B5*   F#5   F#5*   G5   G#5   E9

Intro

D#5 E5   D#5   E5
       Whew! D'ya ever ____ seem to have

       D#5   E5
One of those days when everyone's on your case,

       D#5   E5   D#5
From your teacher all the way down to your best girl-friend?

E5   D#5   E5   D#5
    Well, you know, I used to have ____ 'em just about all the time,

E5   D#5 E5   D#5
But I found a way to get out of it. Let me tell you about…

Verse 1

E5 D#5 E5   B5
    I'm   sittin' in the classroom, thinkin' it's a drag.

C5   B5 C5
Listenin' to the teacher rap ____   just ain't my bag.

    D#5 E5
But when two bells ring, you know it's my cue.

B5 C5   B5 C5
I'm gonna meet the boys on ____   floor number two.

Chorus 1

A5
Smokin' in the boys room.

E5*
Smokin' in the boys room.

      B5*   A5
Now, teach - er, don't fill me up with your rules,

     B5*
'Cause ev'rybody knows that

A5   D$\sharp$5 E5   D$\sharp$5 E5 D$\sharp$5
Smokin' ain't allowed in ____ school.

Verse 2

E5   B5
Checkin' out the hall, makin' sure the coast is clear.

C5   B5   C5   D$\sharp$5
Lookin' in the stalls, nah, there ain't nobody here.

E5
My buddies Sixx, Mick and Tom,

B5 C5   B5 C5
To get caught would surely be the death of us all.

Chorus 2

A5
Smokin' in the boys room.

E5*
Smokin' in the boys room.

      B5*   A5
Now, teach - er, don't fill me up with your rules,

     B5*
'Cause ev'rybody knows that

A5   D$\sharp$5 E5
Smokin' ain't allowed in ____ school.

Hey, can I be excused?

Harp Solo | A5 | | E5* | |
                 | A5 | | B5* | |

Guitar Solo | A5 | | E5* | |
                 | A5 | | B5* | |
                 | A5 | | E5* | |
                 | F$\sharp$5 | B5

Verse 3

D#5 E5   D#5 E5   B5
Well, ____ put me to work in the   school book store,

C5   B5 C5   D#5
Checkout counter, and I _____ got bored.

E5   D#5 E5   B5
Teacher was lookin' for   me all around.

C5   B5 C5
Two hours later, you know where I was found.

Chorus 3

A5
Smokin' in the boys room.

E5*
Smokin' in the boys room.

        B5*   A5
Now, teach - er, don't fill me up with your rules,

        B5*
'Cause ev'rybody knows that

A5   D#5 E5   F#5* G5 G#5
 Smokin' ain't allowed in ____   school.

Outro

N.C.
Smokin' in the boys room. Smokin' in the boys room.

I tell you, I was smoking' in the boys room.

Smokin' in the boys room.

        B5*   A5
Hey, teach - er, don't ya fill me up with your rules,

        B5*
'Cause ev'rybody knows that

A5   D#5 E5   F#5* G5 G#5
Smokin' ain't allowed in ____   school.

A5
Smokin' in the boys room.

E5*
Smokin in the boys room.

        B5*   A5
Now, teach-er, I ain't foolin' a-round with your rules,

        B5*
'Cause ev'rybody knows that

A5   E9
Smokin' ain't allowed in school.

(She's) Some Kind of Wonderful

Words and Music
by John Ellison

D   G   A   Bm

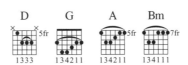

Intro |D | | | |

Verse 1
       D
I don't need a whole lots of money.

I don't need a big fine car.

I got ev'rything that a man could want.

I got more than I could ask for.

G
   I, I don't have to run around.

I don't have to stay out all night.

            D
'Cause I got me a sweet, a sweet lovin' woman

And she knows just how to treat me right.

         A
Well, my ba - by, she's all right.

         G
Well, my ba - by, she's clean out of sight.

Chorus 1
                                           D   **G**
Don't you know that she's,   she's some kind of wonderful.

D   **G**
   She's some kind of wonderful.

                  D   **G**
Yeah, she is, she's, she's some kind of wonderful.

                  D
Yeah, yeah, yeah, yeah.

Verse 2
D
When I hold her in my arms

You know she sets my soul on fire.

Ooh, when my baby kisses me

My heart becomes filled with desire.

          G
When she wraps her lovin' arms around me

It 'bout drives me out of my mind.

          D
Yeah, ___ when my baby kisses me

Chills run up and down my spine.

             A
Well, my ba - by, she's all right.

             G
Well, my ba - by, she's clean out of sight.

Chorus 2
                                D   **G**
Don't you know that she is some kind of wonderful.

D   **G**
   She's some kind of wonderful.

                  D   **G**
Yeah, she is, she's, she's some kind of wonderful.

                  D
Yeah, yeah, yeah, yeah.

Bridge

D

Now, is there anybody got a sweet little woman like mine?

There's got to be somebody got a, got a sweet little woman like mine.

Yeah. Now, can I get a witness?

　　　　　Bm　　　　　　　　　D
Can I get a witness? Well, can I get a witness?

　　　　　Bm　　　　　　　D
Can I get a witness? Can I get a witness?

　　　　　Bm
Can I get a witness?

Outro

　　　　　　　　　　　　　　　　D
I'm talkin', talkin' 'bout my baby.

　　　　　　　G
(She's some kind of wonderful.)

Talkin' 'bout my baby.

　　　　　　　D
(She's some kind of wonderful.)

‖: Talkin' 'bout my baby.

　　　　　　　G
(She's some kind of wonderful.)

Talkin' 'bout my baby.

　　　　　　　D
(She's some kind of wonderful.) :‖ *Repeat and fade*
(w/voc. ad lib.)

Start Me Up

Words and Music by
Mick Jagger and Keith Richards

Open G tuning:
(low to high) D–G–D–G–B–D

Melody:

If you start me up,

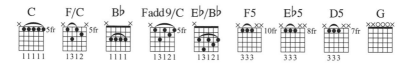

C   F/C   B♭   Fadd9/C   E♭/B♭   F5   E♭5   D5   G

Intro

C| F/C C |F/C C F/C |B♭ | C |

|F/C Fadd9/C C |Fadd9/C F/C C Fadd9/C |

|B♭ E♭/B♭ B♭| E♭/B♭ B♭ |

Verse 1

    C F/C C
If you start me up,

Fadd9/C F/C C   **Fadd9/C B♭**
   If you start me up, I'll never stop.

     C F/C C F/C
If you start me up,

    C F/C   B♭
 If you start me up, I'll never stop.

    C F/C   C
I'll be runnin' hot, uh.

F/C **C**   **F/C**   **B♭**
The job we're rig-gin', now, don't blow my top.

C   **F/C**   **C F/C**
If you start me up, uh,

   C **Fadd9/C B♭**
If you start me up, I'll never stop,

Never stop, never stop, I'll never stop.

Chorus 1

C   F5
You make a grown man ___ cry.

C   F5
You make a grown man ___ cry.

C   F5
You make a grown man ___ cry.

C   F/C   C   F/C C
Spread out the oil, the gaso-line.

                              E♭5   D5 E♭5
I want a smooth ride in a mean,

D5   C Fadd9/C C F/C
Mean machine.

B♭   E♭ B♭
Start it up.

Verse 2

        C   F/C   C
You can start me up.

F/C   B♭
Kick on the starter, give it all you've got,

You've got, you've got.

 C F/C   C Fadd9/C C   B♭
I can compete   with the riders in the other heats.

      C   F/C C Fadd9/C
If you rough it up,   'n'

F/C C   Fadd9/C
If   you like it,

      B♭
You can start it up, start it up, start it up, start it up.

Chorus 2

       C   D5   F5   E♭5 D5 C
Don't make a grown ____ man ____ cry.

                            D   F5   E♭5 D5 C
Don't make a grown man ____ cry.

                       D5 F5   E♭5 C
Don't make a grown man ____ cry.

Fadd9/C C   Fadd9/C C
My eyes   dilate, my lips   go green.

My hands are greasy,

          E♭5 D5 E♭5 D5   C F/C C F/C C F/C
She's a mean, ____ mean machine.

B♭
Start it up.

Verse 3

         C   Fadd9/C C
Mm, ____ start me up.

Fadd9/C C F/C   B♭
  Now, _____ give it all you got,

You've got to never, never, never stop.

C F/C   C
Start it up. Whoo!

F/C C   F/C   B♭
Oh, ____ ba-by, why don't ya start it up?

                 C
Never, never, nev-er.

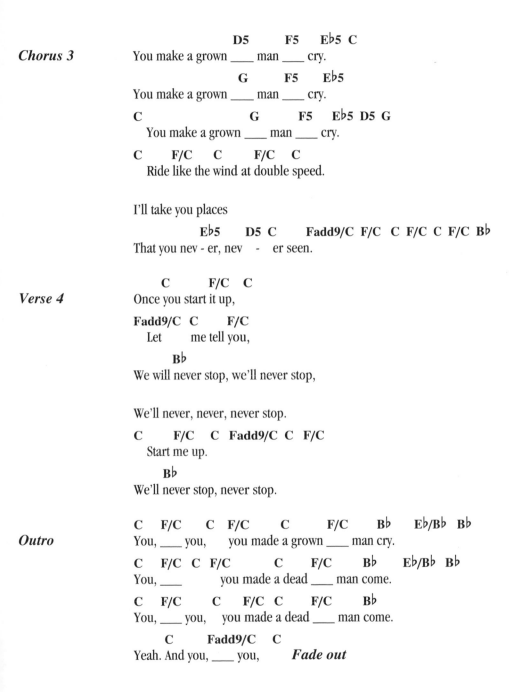

Chorus 3

                      D5   F5   Eb5 C
You make a grown ____ man ____ cry.

                     G   F5   Eb5
You make a grown ____ man ____ cry.

C   **G**   **F5**   **Eb5 D5 G**
  You make a grown ____ man ____ cry.

C   **F/C**   **C**   **F/C**   **C**
  Ride like the wind at double speed.

I'll take you places

              Eb5   **D5 C**   **Fadd9/C F/C C F/C C F/C Bb**
That you nev - er, nev - er seen.

         C   **F/C**   **C**

Verse 4

Once you start it up,

Fadd9/C C   **F/C**
  Let   me tell you,

       Bb
We will never stop, we'll never stop,

We'll never, never, never stop.

C   **F/C**   **C Fadd9/C C F/C**
  Start me up.

       Bb
We'll never stop, never stop.

     C **F/C**   **C** **F/C**   **C**   **F/C**   **Bb**   **Eb/Bb Bb**

Outro

You, ____ you,   you made a grown ____ man cry.
     C **F/C** **C F/C**   **C**   **F/C**   **Bb**   **Eb/Bb Bb**
You, ____   you made a dead ____ man come.
     C **F/C**   **C** **F/C C**   **F/C**   **Bb**
You, ____ you,   you made a dead ____ man come.
        C   **Fadd9/C**   **C**
Yeah. And you, ____ you,   ***Fade out***

Still the Same

Words and Music
by Bob Seger

Melody:

You al - ways won

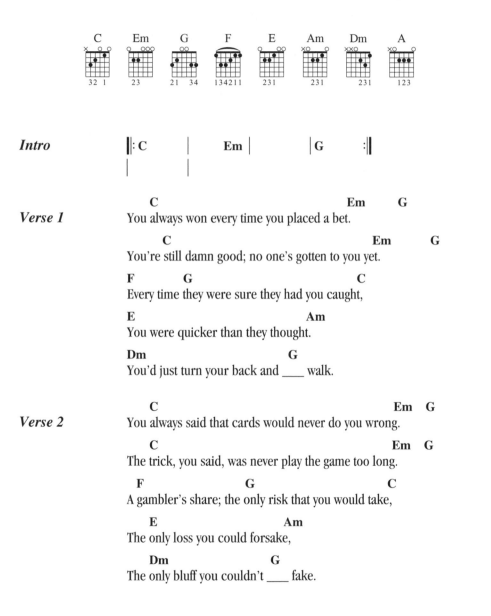

C   Em   G   F   E   Am   Dm   A

32 1   23   21 34   134211   231   231   231   123

Intro
‖: C | Em | | G :‖
| |

Verse 1

    C   Em   G
You always won every time you placed a bet.

        C   Em   G
You're still damn good; no one's gotten to you yet.

F   G   C
Every time they were sure they had you caught,

E   Am
You were quicker than they thought.

Dm   G
You'd just turn your back and ___ walk.

Verse 2

    C   Em   G
You always said that cards would never do you wrong.

    C   Em   G
The trick, you said, was never play the game too long.

  F   G   C
A gambler's share; the only risk that you would take,

  E   Am
The only loss you could forsake,

  Dm   G
The only bluff you couldn't ___ fake.

Chorus 1
                                         C
And you're still the same.

      E   **A**
I caught up with you yesterday.

                     Dm
Moving game to game;

                              G
No one standing in your way.

                    C
Turning on the charm

E   **A**
Long enough to get you by.

                     Dm   **G**
You're still the same, ___ you still aim ___ high.

Piano Solo
‖: C | | Em | G :‖

Verse 3
F   **G**   **C**
There you stood; ev'rybody watched you play.

E   **Am**
I just turned and walked away.

Dm   **G**
I had nothing left to say.

	C
Chorus 2	'Cause you're still the same.

                                                                             Em   G

(Still the same, baby, babe, you're still the same.)

                  C

You're still the same.

                                                                                  Em   G

(Still the same, baby, babe, you're still the same.)

                       C

Moving game to game.

                                                                             Em   G

(Still the same, baby, babe, you're still the same.)

                           C

Some things never change.

                                                                            Em   G

(Still the same, baby, babe, you're still the same.)

                       C

Ah, you're still the same.

                                                                             Em   G

(Still the same, baby, babe, you're still the same.)

                     C

Still the same.

                                                                             Em   G

(Still the same, baby, babe, you're still the same.)   *Fade out*

Stray Cat Strut

Words and Music
by Brian Setzer

Melody:

Black ___ and or - ange stray cat

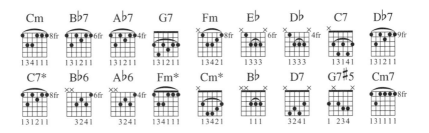

Cm Bb7 Ab7 G7 Fm Eb Db C7 Db7

C7* Bb6 Ab6 Fm* Cm* Bb D7 G7#5 Cm7

Intro
```
| N.C.           |              |              |
||: (C5) (Bb5) | (Ab5) (G5) :||
||: Cm  Bb7  | Ab7   G7  | Cm  Bb7  | Ab7  G7  :||
```

    Cm   Bb7   Ab7   G7   Cm Bb7 Ab7 G7

Verse 1   Black and orange stray cat sittin' on a fence.

    Cm   Bb7   Ab7 G7   Cm Bb7 Ab7 G7

Ain't got e-nough dough to pay the rent.

        Cm   Bb7   Ab7   G7

I'm ___ flat broke but I don't care,

     Cm N.C.

I strut right by with my tail in the air.

Chorus

Fm   E♭   D♭   C7
Stay cat strut, I'm a (Ladies' cat.)

     Fm   E♭   D♭7   C7*
I'm a feline Casa-nova. (Hey! Man, that's sad.)

     Fm   E♭   D♭7   C7*
Get a shoe thrown at me from a mean old man.

Fm N.C.
Get my dinner from a garbage can.

Interlude 1

|Cm B♭7 |A♭7 G7 |Cm B♭7 |A♭7   G7 |
              Yeah.   Yeah, don't cross ___ my path!

Guitar Solo 1

|Cm B♭7 |A♭7 G7 |Cm B♭7 |A♭7 G7 |
|Cm B♭6 |A♭6 G7 |Cm N.C. |

Bridge 1

Fm   Fm*   Cm*
I don't bother chasin' mice around.

          B♭ Fm*
Whoa, no! ___ I slink down the alley, lookin' for a fight,

     D7   G7
Howl-in' to the moonlight on a hot summer night.

Verse 2

     Cm   B♭7   A♭7   G7
Sing - in' the blues ___ while the lady cats cry,

      Cm   B♭7   A♭7   G7
"Wild ___ stray cat, you're a real gone guy."

   Cm   B♭7 A♭7   G7
I wish I could be as carefree and wild,

     Cm N.C.
But I got cat class and I got cat style.

Interlude 2 |Cm B♭7 |A♭7 G7 |Cm B♭7 |A♭7 G7 |
              |Cm |A♭7 G7♯5 |Cm |A♭7 G7♯5 |
              |Cm |A♭7 G7♯5 |Cm |A♭7 G7 |

Guitar Solo 2 |Cm B♭7 |A♭7 G7 |Cm B♭7 |A♭7 G7 |
                |Cm B♭7 |A♭7 G7 |Cm N.C. | |

Bridge 2

  Fm   Cm
I don't bother chasin' mice around.

   Fm*
I slink down the alley, lookin' for a fight,

    D7   G7
Howl - in' to the moonlight on a hot summer night.

Verse 3

      Cm   B♭7   A♭7   G7
Sing - in' the blues ___ while the lady cats cry,

        Cm   B♭7   A♭7   G7
"Wild ___ stray cat, you're a real gone guy."

  Cm   B♭7 A♭7   G7
I wish I could be as carefree and wild,

     Cm N.C.
But I got cat class and I got cat style.

Outro |N.C. | |
      | | Cm7| | | |
                   Yow!

The Stroke

Words and Music
by Billy Squier

Now, ev - 'ry-bod - y,   ah,   have you heard? ____

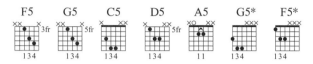

F5   G5   C5   D5   A5   G5*   F5*

Intro

| N.C. | | |

Verse 1

N.C.
Now, ev'rybody, ah, have you heard?

If you're in the game, ah, then stroke's the word.

Pre-Chorus 1

F5 G5 N.C.   C5 D5
       Don't take no rhythm,

N.C.   F5 G5
   Don't take no style.

N.C.
   Got a thirst for killin'.

A5   N.C.(G5)   (F5) (E5) D5   C5 G5 D5 G5
      Grab your vial   and...   Whew!

Verse 2

F5   D5 N.C.   D5 N.C.
Put your right hand out,

     D5 N.C.   G5* F5*
Give a firm handshake.

D5 N.C.   D5 N.C.
Talk to me

     D5 N.C.
About that one big break.

	F5* G5* N.C. C5 D5
Pre-Chorus 2	Spread your ear pollution

N.C.   F5* G5*

Both far and wide.

N.C.   A5

Keep your contributions

N.C. (G5)   (F5)   (E5)

By your side   and…

	C5 D5 N.C. D5 N.C.
Chorus 1	Stroke me, stroke me.

Could be a winner, boy,

  G5*   F5*

And move quite ah, well.

C5   D5 N.C.   D5 N.C. G5* F5*

Stroke me, stroke me.

C5   D5 N.C.   D5 N.C.

Stroke me, stroke me.

                  G5*   F5*

You got your number down.

C5   D5 N.C.   D5 N.C.

Stroke me, stroke me.

Say you're a winner.

             D5 N.C.   D5 N.C.

Man, you're just a sinner now.

Interlude	| D5 N.C. C5 G5* |
	| D5 N.C. D N.C. | D5 N.C. G5* F5* |

Verse 3

            D5 N.C.   D5 N.C.
Put your left foot out,

              D5   N.C.   G5* F5*
Ah, keep it all in place.

D5   N.C.   D5 N.C.
Work your way

        D5 N.C.
 Right into my place.

Pre-Chorus 3

F5* G5* N.C.   C5   D5
              First you try to bet me,

N.C.   F5* G5*
You make my back bone slide.

N.C.   A5
Ah, when you find you've bled me,

N.C. (G5)   (F5) (E5)
     Slip on by.   Keep on…

Chorus 2

C5   D5 N.C.   D5 N.C.
 Stroke me, stroke me.

              G5*   F5*
Give me the business all ___ night long.

C5   D5 N.C.   D5 N.C.   G5* F5*
Stroke me, stroke me.

C5   D5 N.C.   D5 N.C.
Stroke me, stroke me.

              G5*   F5*
You're so together, boy.

C5   D5 N.C.   D5 N.C.
Stroke me, stroke me.

Say you're a winner, but man,

              D5
You're just a sinner now.

Breakdown

N.C.
Yelled: (Stroke! Stroke! Stroke! Stroke! Stroke! Stroke! Stroke!)

| D5 N.C.   D5   N.C. | D5 N.C.   C5* G5* |

| D5 N.C.   D5   N.C. | D5 N.C.   G5* F5* |

Verse 4

       D5   N.C.   **D5** N.C.
Better listen now,

       D5 N.C.   **G5*** **F5***
I said it ain't no joke.

         D5 N.C.   **D5** N.C.
Don't let your con-science fail ya,

     D5   N.C.
Just do the stroke.

Pre-Chorus 4

F5* **G5*** N.C.   **C5** **D5**
      Don't you take no chances,

N.C.   **F5*** **G5***
  Keep your eye on top.

N.C.   **A5**
  Do your fancy dances.

N.C. **(G5)**   **(F5)** **(E5)**
  You can't stop,   you just…

Chorus 3

C5   **D5** N.C.
Stroke me, stroke me. (Stroke! Stroke!)

Stroke me, stroke me. (Stroke! Stroke!)

Stroke me, stroke me.(Stroke! Stroke!)

                              C5 **G5***
Stroke me, stroke me. (Stroke!) Do it!

C5   **D5** N.C.   **D5** N.C.   **C5** **G5***
Stroke me, stroke me.   (Stroke!)

C5   **D5** N.C.   **D5**   N.C.   **C5** **F5***
Stroke me, stroke me. Keep on!   (Stroke!)

C5   **D5** N.C.   **D5**   N.C.   **C5** **G5***
Stroke me, stroke me. Hey, you're gonna (Stroke!)

C5   **D5** N.C.   **D5** N.C.
Stroke me, stroke me.

Say you're a winner, man, you're just a sinner now.

Sunshine of Your Love

Words and Music by Jack Bruce,
Pete Brown and Eric Clapton

Melody:

It's get-ting near dawn, _

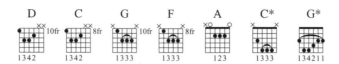

Intro

‖: N.C.(D) | :‖

‖: D   C D N.C. | :‖

Verse 1

        D   C   D   N.C.
It's getting near dawn,

         D   C   D N.C.
When lights close their tired   eyes.

        D   C D N.C.
I'll soon be with you, ___ my love,

        D   C D N.C.
To give you my dawn _____ surprise.

        G   F G N.C.
I'll be with you, dar - ling, soon.

        G   F G N.C.
I'll be with you when   the stars start falling.

| D   C D N.C. | | D   C D N.C. | |

Chorus 1

> A N.C.   C*   G*
> I've been wait - ing so __ long
>
> A N.C.   C*   G*
> To be where __ I'm go - ing
>
> A N.C.   C/G   G*   A
> In the sun - shine of __ your love.
>
> |D   C D N.C. | |

Verse 2

>   D   C D N.C.
> I'm with you, my love;
>
>   D   C D   N.C.
> The light shin-ing through ___ on you.
>
>   D   C D N.C.
> Yes, I'm with you, my love.
>
>   D   C D N.C.
> It's the morning and just ___ we two.
>
>   G   F   G N.C.
> I'll stay with you, dar - ling, now.
>
>   G   F G N.C.
> I'll stay with you till my seeds are dried up.
>
> |D C D N.C. | |D   C D N.C. | |

Chorus 2

> A N.C.   C*   G
> I've been wait - ing so __ long
>
> A N.C.   C*   G
> To be where __ I'm go - ing
>
> A N.C.   C*   G   A
> In the sun - shine of __ your love.

Guitar Solo

```
|D   C D N.C. |          |D   C D N.C. |          |
|D   C D N.C. |          |D   C D N.C. |          |
|G   F G N.C. |          |G   F G N.C. |          |
|D   C D N.C. |          |D   C D N.C. |          |
|A           |C*  G  |A              |C*  G  |
|A           |C*  G  |A              |       |
|D   C D N.C. |          |D   C D N.C. |          |
```

Verse 3   *Repeat Verse 2*

Outro

   A N.C.   C*   G
     I've been wait - ing so ____ long,

   A N.C.   C*   G
     I've been wait - ing so ____ long,

   A N.C.   C*   G
     I've been wait - ing so ____ long,

   A N.C.   C*   G
     To be where ____ I'm go - ing

   A N.C.   C*   G   A
     In the sun - shine of ____ your love.

   ‖: A | **:‖** *Repeat and fade*

Take Me to the River

Words and Music by
Al Green and Mabon Hodges

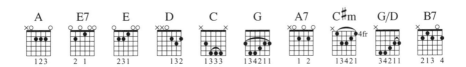

Intro

A	E7		A	E7		
E A E7	A E7			
E A E7	A E7		D A

Verse 1

E7   D A
 I don't know why I love you like I do,

E7   D A
 After all these changes that you put me through.

E7   D A
 You stole my money and my cigarettes,

E7   D
 And I haven't seen hide nor hair of you yet.

A C   G   D   A7
I wanna know. Won't you tell me, am I in love to stay?

(Take me, take me.)

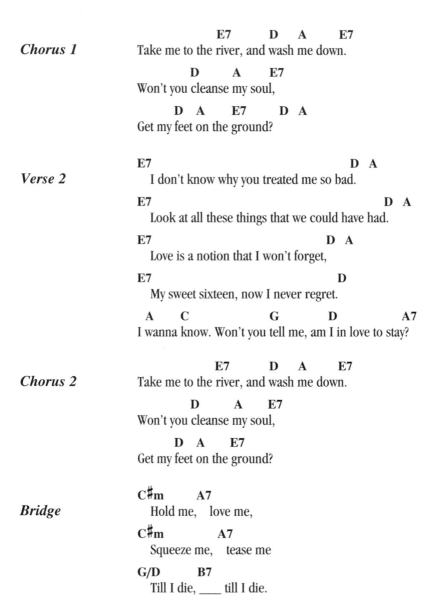

Chorus 1

                  E7   **D**   **A**   **E7**
Take me to the river, and wash me down.

         D   **A**   **E7**
Won't you cleanse my soul,

      D **A**   **E7**   **D** **A**
Get my feet on the ground?

Verse 2

E7   **D** **A**
I don't know why you treated me so bad.

E7   **D** **A**
Look at all these things that we could have had.

E7   **D** **A**
Love is a notion that I won't forget,

E7   **D**
My sweet sixteen, now I never regret.

      A   **C**   **G**   **D**   **A7**
I wanna know. Won't you tell me, am I in love to stay?

Chorus 2

                  E7   **D**   **A**   **E7**
Take me to the river, and wash me down.

         D   **A**   **E7**
Won't you cleanse my soul,

      D **A**   **E7**
Get my feet on the ground?

Bridge

C♯m   **A7**
Hold me,   love me,

C♯m   **A7**
Squeeze me,   tease me

G/D   **B7**
Till I die, ___ till I die.

Chorus 3   Take me, baby,

        E7   **D** **A** **E7**
       Take me to the river, and wash me down.

        D   **A** **E7**
       Won't you cleanse my soul,

        D **A** **E7** **D A**
       Get my feet on the ground?

Verse 3   *Repeat Verse 1*

        E7   **D** **A** **E7**
Chorus 4   Take me to the river, and wash me down.

        D   **A** **E7**
       Won't you cleanse my soul,

        D **A** **E7**
       Get my feet on the ground?

      D **A**   **E7** **D** **A**   **E7**
      Yeah, ___ yeah, ___ yeah, ___ yeah, ___ yeah.

       D **A** **E7**
Outro   ‖: Dip me in the water,

      D **A** **E7**
      Dip me in the water, baby. :‖ *Play 3 times*

      | **D A** |**E7**

Sweet Emotion

Words and Music by
Steven Tyler and Tom Hamilton

Melody:

Sweet _____ e - mo - tion.

D/A　A5　D　A　E　E7　E5

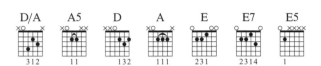

Intro

N.C.(A)			(D/A)		
(A)			(D/A)	D/A	
	A5			D/A		
	N.C.(A)		

Chorus 1

N.C.(A)　(D/A)　(A)
Sweet e - mo - tion.

(D/A)(A)
Sweet e - mo - tion.

Verse 1

A5　　　　　　　　　　　　　　　D　A
Talk about things and nobody cares,

　　　　　D　　　A　　　　　　　　　　　　　D　A
You're wearin' out things that nobody wears.

　　　　　D　　　A　　　　　　　　　　　　　　　D　A
You're callin' my name, but I gotta make clear,

　　　D　A　　　　　　　　　　　　D　A
I can't say, baby, where I'll be in a year.

Interlude 1

‖: N.C. | :‖

Verse 2

        D   A   D   A
Some sweet talking mama with a face like a gent

            D   A   D   A
Said my get up and go must've got up and went.

            D   A   D   A
Well, I got good news, she's a real good liar,

               D   A   D   A
'Cause my back-stage boogie, set yo' pants on fire.

Interlude 2   ‖: N.C. | :‖ *Play 4 times*

Chorus 2   *Repeat Chorus 1*

                 A5   D   A
Verse 3   I pulled into town in a police car,

            D   A   D   A
Your daddy said I took you just a little too far.

              D   A   D   A
You're tellin' her things but your girlfriend lied,

            D   A   D   A
You can't catch me 'cause the rabbit done died.

Yes, it did!

Interlude 3   *Repeat Interlude 1*

                 D   A   D   A
Verse 4   You stand in the front just a shakin' yo ass,

            D   A   D   A
I'll take you backstage, you can drink from my glass.

            D   A   D   A
I'm talkin' 'bout somethin' you can sure understand,

              D   A   D   A
'Cause a month on the road and I'll be eatin' from your hand.

Interlude 4   ‖: N.C. | | | | :‖
                 | E | E7 | | |

Guitar Solo   ‖: E5 | | | :‖ *Repeat and fade*

Take the Long Way Home

Words and Music by
Rick Davies and Roger Hodgson

Melody:

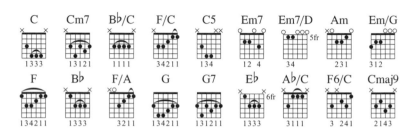

So you think you're a Ro-me-o ____ play-ing a part in a

C	Cm7	B♭/C	F/C	C5	Em7	Em7/D	Am	Em/G
1333	13121	1111	34211	134	12 4	34	231	312

F	B♭	F/A	G	G7	E♭	A♭/C	F6/C	Cmaj9
134211	1333	3211	134211	131211	1333	3111	3 241	2143

Intro
```
|C          |          |          |
||: Cm7  B♭/C |F/C    C  |B♭/C      |C5         :||
```

Verse 1

    Cm7   **B♭/C**
So you think you're a Romeo

F/C   **C**
Playing a part in a picture show,

          B♭/C
Well, take the long way home,

      C5
Take the long way home.

Cm7   **B♭/C**
'Cause you're the joke of the neighborhood,

F/C   **C**
Why should you care if you're feeling good?

          B♭/C
Well, take the long way home,

      C5
Take the long way home.

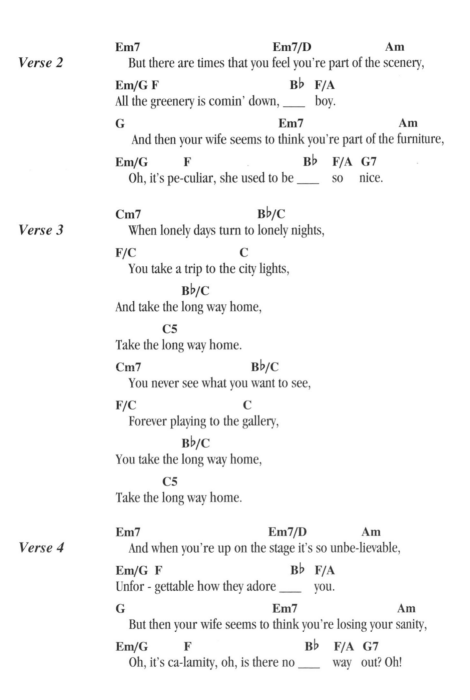

Verse 2

Em7   Em7/D   Am
 But there are times that you feel you're part of the scenery,

Em/G F   B♭ F/A
All the greenery is comin' down, ____ boy.

G   Em7   Am
 And then your wife seems to think you're part of the furniture,

Em/G F   B♭ F/A G7
 Oh, it's pe-culiar, she used to be ____ so nice.

Verse 3

Cm7   B♭/C
 When lonely days turn to lonely nights,

F/C   C
 You take a trip to the city lights,

   B♭/C
And take the long way home,

   C5
Take the long way home.

Cm7   B♭/C
 You never see what you want to see,

F/C   C
 Forever playing to the gallery,

   B♭/C
You take the long way home,

   C5
Take the long way home.

Verse 4

Em7   Em7/D   Am
 And when you're up on the stage it's so unbe-lievable,

Em/G F   B♭ F/A
Unfor - gettable how they adore ____ you.

G   Em7   Am
 But then your wife seems to think you're losing your sanity,

Em/G F   B♭ F/A G7
 Oh, it's ca-lamity, oh, is there no ____ way out? Oh!

Interlude　‖: E♭　B♭　| F　C　| B♭/C　| C5　:‖

Verse 5

Em7　　　　　　　Em7/D　　　Am
　Does it feel that your life's become a ca-tastrophe?

Em/G　F　　　　　　　　　B♭　F/A
Oh, it　has to be, for you to grow, ___　boy.

G　　　　　　　　　Em7　　　　Am
　When you look through the years and see what you could have been,

Em/G　　　F
Oh, what you might have been,

　　　　　　B♭　F/A　G7
If you'd had ___　more time.

Cm7　　　　　　　　B♭/C
　So, when the day comes to settle down,

F/C　　　　　　　　　C
　Well, who's to blame if you're not around?

Chorus

　　　　　　B♭/C　　　　　　　A♭/C
You took the long way home, you took the long way home.

　　　　　F/C　　　　　　B♭/C
You took the long way home, you took the long way home.

　　　A♭/C　　　　　　　F/C
You took the long way home, you took the long way home.

　　　B♭/C　　　　　　　F/C
You took the long way home, you took the long way home.

Outro

‖: F6/C　　| Cmaj9　:‖ *Play 3 times*
　Ah,　　　ah.

B♭/C　　　A♭/C　　　F/C
Long way home, long way home, long way home.

B♭/C　　　A♭/C　　　F/C　　　B♭/C
Long way home, long way home, long way home.

Takin' Care of Business

Words and Music
by Randy Bachman

Melody:

They get up ev - 'ry morn-ing

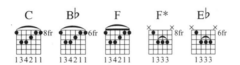

Intro   ‖: C   B♭ | F | C | :‖ *Play 4 times*

               C   B♭

Verse 1   They get up ev'ry morning from the alarm clock's warning.

               F   C
Take the eight fifteen into the city.

                                B♭
There's a whistle up above and peo-ple pushing, people shoving,

               F   C
And the girls who try to look pretty.

                             B♭
And if your train's on time you can get to work by nine

               F   C
And start your slaving job to get your pay.

                           B♭
If you ever get annoyed, look at me, I'm self-employed.

             F   C
I love to work at nothing all day.

Chorus 1

```
C                                    Bb
And I've been taking care of business   ev'ry day,

F                    C
Taking care of business    ev'ry way.

                              Bb
I've been taking care of business,    it's all mine.

F                              C
Taking care of business and working overtime, work out.
```

Interlude 1   ‖: C   Bb | | F   C | :‖

Verse 2

```
C                                    Bb
There's work easy as fishing, you could be a musician,

   F                      C
If you could make sounds loud and mellow.

                         Bb
Get a second hand guitar, chanc-es are you'll go far

      F                        C
If you get in with the right bunch of fellows.

                         Bb
People see you having fun just a lying in the sun.

F                      C
Tell them that you like it this way.

                         Bb
It's the work that we avoid and we're all self-employed.

      F                        C
We love to work at nothing all day.
```

Chorus 2

```
C                                    Bb
And we've been taking care of business    ev'ry day,

F                    C
Taking care of business     ev'ry way.

                              Bb
We've been taking care of business,    it's all mine.

F                    C
Taking care of business and working overtime.
```

Guitar Solo 1   *Repeat Interlude 1*

Interlude 2
C
  Whoa! Alright. Ow.

Bridge   C | F* Eb | Bb C | F* Eb | Bb
            C   F*   Eb   Bb
    Take good care ____ of my business
                 C   F*   Eb Bb
    When I'm a-way,   ev'ry-day. ____ Whoa!

Guitar Solo 2   ‖: C   Bb | | F | C :‖

Verse 3   *Repeat Verse 1*

Chorus 3   *Repeat Chorus 1*

Breakdown
N.C.
Taking care of business. Whoa. Taking care of business.

C   Bb
Taking care of business   ev'ry day.

F   C
Taking care of business   ev'ry way.

                        Bb
Taking care of business,   it's all mine.

F   C
Taking care of business,   working overtime.

Outro
C   Bb
Taking care of business.

F   C
Taking care of business.

                        Bb
We've been taking care of business.

               F   C
We've been taking care of business.   ***Repeat and fade***

Take the Money and Run

Words and Music by
Steve Miller

Melody:

This here's a sto-ry 'bout

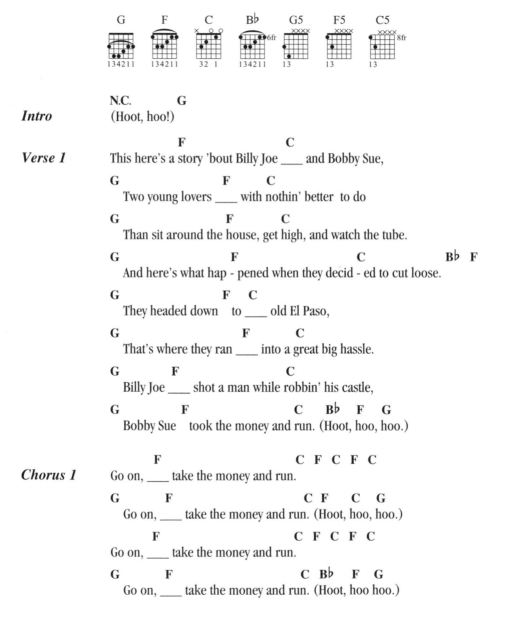

| G | F | C | B♭ | G5 | F5 | C5 |

Intro

N.C.   G
(Hoot, hoo!)

Verse 1

                  F   C
This here's a story 'bout Billy Joe ___ and Bobby Sue,

G   F   C
Two young lovers ___ with nothin' better to do

G   F   C
Than sit around the house, get high, and watch the tube.

G   F   C   B♭ F
And here's what hap - pened when they decid - ed to cut loose.

G   F C
They headed down   to ___ old El Paso,

G   F   C
That's where they ran ___ into a great big hassle.

G   F   C
Billy Joe ___ shot a man while robbin' his castle,

G   F   C B♭ F G
Bobby Sue took the money and run. (Hoot, hoo, hoo.)

Chorus 1

                F   C F C F C
Go on, ___ take the money and run.

G   F   C F   C G
Go on, ___ take the money and run. (Hoot, hoo, hoo.)

                F   C F C F C
Go on, ___ take the money and run.

G   F   C B♭ F G
Go on, ___ take the money and run. (Hoot, hoo hoo.)

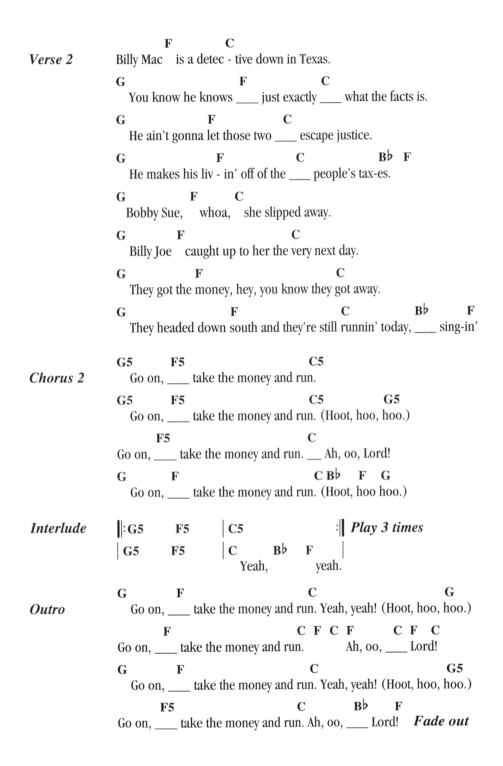

Verse 2

          F   C
Billy Mac   is a detec - tive down in Texas.

G   F   C
You know he knows ___ just exactly ___ what the facts is.

G   F   C
He ain't gonna let those two ___ escape justice.

G   F   C   B♭ F
He makes his liv - in' off of the ___ people's tax-es.

G   F   C
Bobby Sue,   whoa,   she slipped away.

G   F   C
Billy Joe   caught up to her the very next day.

G   F   C
They got the money, hey, you know they got away.

G   F   C   B♭   F
They headed down south and they're still runnin' today, ___ sing-in'

Chorus 2

G5   F5   C5
Go on, ___ take the money and run.

G5   F5   C5   G5
Go on, ___ take the money and run. (Hoot, hoo, hoo.)

          F5   C
Go on, ___ take the money and run. __ Ah, oo, Lord!

G   F   C B♭   F   G
Go on, ___ take the money and run. (Hoot, hoo hoo.)

Interlude   ‖: G5   F5 | C5   :‖ *Play 3 times*

              | G5   F5 | C   B♭   F |
                             Yeah,   yeah.

Outro

G   F   C   G
Go on, ___ take the money and run. Yeah, yeah! (Hoot, hoo, hoo.)

          F   C F C F   C F   C
Go on, ___ take the money and run.   Ah, oo, ___ Lord!

G   F   C   G5
Go on, ___ take the money and run. Yeah, yeah! (Hoot, hoo, hoo.)

          F5   C   B♭   F
Go on, ___ take the money and run. Ah, oo, ___ Lord! *Fade out*

Throwing It All Away

Words and Music by Tony Banks,
Phil Collins and Mike Rutherford

Melody:

Need I say _ I love _ you?

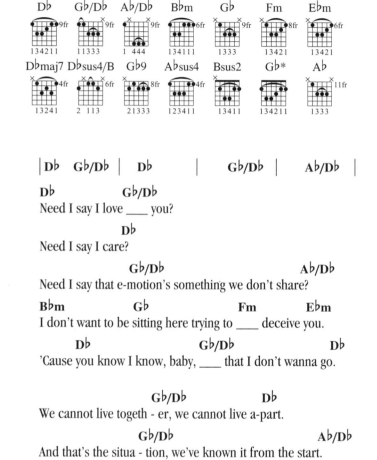

Db   Gb/Db   Ab/Db   Bbm   Gb   Fm   Ebm
Dbmaj7   Dbsus4/B   Gb9   Absus4   Bsus2   Gb*   Ab

Intro

| Db   Gb/Db | Db | Gb/Db | Ab/Db |

Verse 1

    Db   Gb/Db
Need I say I love ____ you?

             Db
Need I say I care?

             Gb/Db   Ab/Db
Need I say that e-motion's something we don't share?

Bbm   Gb   Fm   Ebm
I don't want to be sitting here trying to ____ deceive you.

          Db   Gb/Db   Db
'Cause you know I know, baby, ____ that I don't wanna go.

Verse 2

                Gb/Db   Db
We cannot live togeth - er, we cannot live a-part.

             Gb/Db   Ab/Db
And that's the situa - tion, we've known it from the start.

Bbm   Gb   Fm   Ebm
Ev'ry time that I look at you I can see ____ the fu-ture.

          Db   Gb/Db   Db
'Cause you know I know, baby, ____ that I don't wanna go.

Chorus 1

Dbmaj7 Dbsus4/B   Gb9
                Just throwing it all ____ away,

        Absus4
Throwing it all ____ away.

Dbmaj7 Dbsus4/B   Gb9
                Is there nothing that I can say

    Absus4
To make you change your mind?

Bsus2   Gb*
    I watch the world go 'round and 'round

Bsus2   Gb*
    And see mine turning up - side down.

    Db   Gb/Db
Ooh, ooh. Ooh, ooh.

    Ab/Db   Gb/Db
Ooh, ooh. Ooh, ooh, ooh.

             Db
Throwing it all away.

    Gb/Db   Ab/Db   Gb/Db
Ooh, ooh. Ooh, ooh. Ooh, ooh, ooh.

Verse 3

    Db   Gb/Db
Now who will light up the dark - ness,

             Db
And who will hold your hand?

          Gb/Db
Who will find you the answers

             Ab/Db
When you don't understand?

Bbm   Gb
Why should I have to be the one

        Fm   Ebm
Who has to ____ convince ____ you?

    Db   Gb/Db   Db
'Cause you know I know, baby, ____ that I don't wanna go.

Verse 4

                  Gb/Db   **Db**
Someday you'll be sorry.   Someday when you're free.

          Gb/Db   **Ab/Db**
Memories will re-mind you that our love was meant to be.

  Bbm   **Gb**
But late at night when you call my name,

        Fm   **Ebm**
The only sound you'll hear

    Db   **Ebm** **Gb/Db**   **Db**
Is the sound of your voice calling, calling after me.

Chorus 2

Dbmaj7   **Dbsus4/B**   **Gb9**
             Just throwing it all ____ away,

        Absus4
Throwing it all ____ away.

Dbmaj7   **Dbsus4/B**   **Gb**   **Ab**
          And there's nothing that I can say. Ay. ____ Ah.

Outro

        Db   **Gb/Db**
‖: (Ooh, ____ ooh. Ooh, ooh.

    Ab/Db   **Gb/Db**
Ooh, ooh. Ooh, ooh, ooh.)

              Db
We're throwing it all away. :‖ *Repeat and fade*

Turn Me Loose

Words and Music by
Paul Dean and Duke Reno

Melody:

I was born to run, __ I was

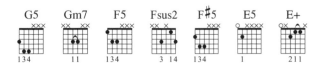

G5   Gm7   F5   Fsus2   F#5   E5   E+

Intro

G5 Gm7		G5 Gm7	
F5 Fsus2	F5 F#5	G5 Gm7	
G5 Gm7	G5		Gm7	
F5		G5 Gm7	

Verse 1

      G5
I was born to run, I was born to dream.

The craziest boy you've ever seen.
   F#5 F5   **F#5**   **G5** **N.C.**
I gotta do it my way, or no way at all.

     G5
And I was here to please, I'm even on my knees

Making love to whoever I please.
   F#5 F5   **F#5**   **G5** **N.C.**
I gotta do it my way, or no way at all.

Verse 2

       G5
And then you came around, tried to tie me down. I was such a clown.
     F#5   **F5**   **F#5**   **G5** **N.C.**
You had to have it your way, or no way at all.

       G5
But I've had all I can take, I can't take it no more.
             F#5   **F5**   **F#5**   **G5**
I'm gonna pack my bags and fly it my ____ way, or no way at all.

Chorus 1

    N.C.   G5
    So why don't you turn me loose?

Turn me loose. Turn me loose.
      F#5 F5   F#5   G5
I gotta do it my way, or no way at all.
N.C.   G5
    Why don't you turn me loose?

Turn me loose. Turn me loose.
       F5   F#5   G5
I've gotta do it my way. I wanna fly.

Interlude 1

‖: E5 | N.C.   :‖ *Play 3 times*
| E5 | E+ |

Verse 3

    G5
I'm here to please, I'm even on my knees

Making love to whoever I please.
     F#5 F5   F#5   G5   N.C.
I've gotta do it my way, I've gotta do it my way.
     G5
And when you come around,

You tried to tie me down, I was such a clown.
    F#5 F5   F#5   G5
You had to have it your way, well, I'm sayin' ___ no way.

Chorus 2

N.C.   G5
    So why don't you turn me loose?

Turn me loose. Turn me loose.
    F#5 F5   F#5   G5
I gotta do it my way, or no way at all.
N.C.   G5
    Why don't you turn me loose?

Turn me loose. Turn me loose.
       F5   F#5   G5 E5 F5 F#5
I've gotta do it my way. I wanna fly.   Oh, yeah.

Interlude 2		G5	Gm7	G5	Gm7	G5	Gm7	G5	Gm7	
		F5	Fsus2		F5	F#5	G5	Gm7		

Guitar Solo

	G5				F#5
	F5		F#5		

Outro

    N.C.   G5
  So why don't you turn me loose?

Turn me loose. Turn me loose.
        F#5 F5   F#5
I've gotta do it my way, or no way at all.

N.C.   G5
  Why don't you turn me loose?

Turn me loose. Turn me loose.
        F#5 F5
I've gotta do it my way.
     F#5   G5
I've gotta do it my way.

N.C.   G5   Gm7
  Why don't you turn me loose?

G5   Gm7 G5   Gm7
Turn me loose.   Turn me loose.

G5   Gm7   F5   G5 F5 F#5   G5 Gm7
  I've gotta do it my ___ way,   I wanna fly.

G5
Turn me loose. Turn me loose. Turn me loose.
        F#5 F5
Turn me loose.   Turn me loose.
        F#5 G5
Turn me loose.   Turn me loose.

Tush

Words and Music by Billy F Gibbons,
Dusty Hill and Frank Beard

Melody:

I've been up, ____

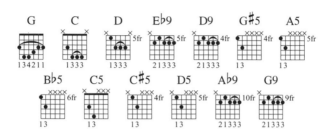

Intro | G | |

            Yeah!

        | | | | |

Verse 1

G
I've been up, I've been down,

                              C
Take my word, my way 'round.

                    G
I ain't askin' for much. ____ Mm.

          D
I said, Lord, ____ take me downtown,

C   G   E♭9 D9
I'm just lookin' for some tush.

Verse 2

                  G
I've been bad, ____ I've been good,

                             C
Dallas, Texas, Hollywood.

                        G
I ain't askin' for much. ____ Mm.

                  D
I said, Lord, ____ take me downtown,

C   G   E♭9 D9
I'm just lookin' for some tush. ____ Yeah.

Guitar Solo

G				G♯5 A5 B♭5
C		G		
D	C	G		C5 C♯5 D5
G				G♯5 A5 B♭5
C		G		
D	C	G		E♭9 D9

Verse 3

                  G
Take me back, way back home,

                          C
Not by myself, not alone.

                        G
I ain't askin' for much. ____ Mm.

                  D
I said, Lord, ____ take me downtown,

C   G
  I'm just lookin' for some tush.

Outro

G				G♯5 A5 B♭5
C		G		
D	C	G N.C.		A♭9 G9

Walk on the Wild Side

Words and Music
by Lou Reed

Melody:

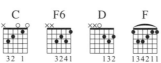

Hol - ly came _ from Mi-am - i, F. L. A., ___

C   F6   D   F

32 1   3241   132   134211

Intro   ‖: C | F6   :‖ *Play 4 times*

Verse 1

C   F6
Holly came from Miami, F.L.A.,

C   F6
Hitchhiked her way across the U.S.A.

C   D
Plucked her eyebrows on ___ the way,

F   D
Shaved her legs and then he was a she.

        C   F6
She says, "Hey babe, take a walk on the wild ___ side."

        C   F6
She says. "Hey honey, take a walk on the wild ___ side."

Verse 2

C   F6
Candy came from out on the island,

C   F6
In the back room she was ev'rybody's darlin'.

C   D
But she never lost ___ her head,

F   D
Even when she was givin' head.

        C   F6
She says, "Hey babe, take a walk on the wild ___ side."

        C   F6
She says, "Hey babe, take a walk on the wild side."

                C
And the colored girls go...

Chorus 1

C
‖: Do, do, do, do, do, do, do, do,

F6
Do, do, do, do, do, do, do, do. :‖

C
‖: (Do, do, do, do, do, do, do, do,

F6
Do, do, do, do, do, do, do, do.) :‖

Interlude 1

| C | F6 | C | F6 | |
Do.

Verse 3

C   F6
Little Joe never once gave it away,

C   F6
Ev'rybody had to pay and pay.

 C   D
A hustle here and a hustle there,

F   D
New York City is the ___ place where they said,

C   F6
"Hey babe, take a walk on the wild side."

          C   F6
They said, "Hey Joe, take a walk on the wild ___ side."

Interlude 2

| C | F6 | C | F6 | |

Verse 4

C   F6
Sugar plum fairies came and hit the streets

C   F6
Looking for soul food and a place to eat.

C   D   F   D
Went to the Apollo, you should have seen them go, ___ go, go.

          C   F6
The said, "Hey sugar, take a walk on the wild side."

          C   F6
They said, "Hey babe, take a walk on the wild ___ side."

          C   F6   C   F6
All right?   Huh.

Verse 5

C   F6
Jackie is just speedin' away.

C   F6
Thought she was James Dean for a day.

C   D
Then I guess she had ___ to crash.

F   D
Valium would've helped that bash.

     C   F6
She said, "Hey babe, take a walk on the wild ___ side."

      C   F6
She said, "Hey Honey, take a walk on the wild ___ side."

And the colored girls sing,

Chorus 2

   C
‖: Do, do, do, do, do, do, do, do,

F6
Do, do, do, do, do, do, do, do. :‖

‖: C
  (Do, do, do, do, do, do, do, do,

F6
Do, do, do, do, do, do, do, do.) :‖ *Play 4 times*

Sax Solo | C | F6 | C | F6 |
       (Do.)

       ‖: C | F6 | C | F6   :‖ *Repeat till fade*

Won't Get Fooled Again

Words and Music
by Pete Townshend

Melody:

We'll be fight-ing in the streets

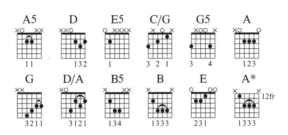

Intro   ‖: A5 | | | :‖

	A5
Verse 1	We'll be fighting in the streets

D   A5
With our children at our feet

D   A5   D   E5
And the morals that they worship will be gone.

C/G G5   A5
And the men who spurred us on

D   A5
Sit in judgement of all wrong,

                        D   E5 C/G G5
They decide and the shotgun sings the song.

Chorus 1

    D   **A**   **D**   **A**
I'll tip my hat to the new consti-tution,

D   **A**   **D**   **A**
Take a bow ___ for the new revo-lution.

D   **A**   **D**   **A**
Smile and grin ___ at the change all a-round,

G5   **E5**
Pick up my guitar and play,

G5   **E5**
Just like yesterday,

       G5   **D** **G**   **D** **G** **D**
Then I'll get on my knees and pray,

            A5   **G5** **D**
We won't get fooled again.   No, no!

Interlude 1 | **A5**   **G** | | **A5** | **D** |
               | **A5** | **D/A** |

Bridge

    B5
I'll move myself and my fam'ly aside,

E5
  If we happen to be left half alive,

   A5
I'll get all my papers and smile at the sky,

    B5
Oh, I know that the hypnotized never lie.

Interlude 2 | **B** | **A** **E** | **B** | **A** **E** |

Guitar Solo | **B** | **A** **E** | **B** | **A** **E** |
              | **B** | **A** **E** | **B** | |

Interlude 3 ||: **A5** | **G5** **D** | **A5** | **G5** **D** :||
                Yeah!

Verse 2

       A5
There's nothing in the street

D   A5
Looks any different to me.

G5 D   A5   G5 D   E
And the slogans are replaced by ___ the by.

C/G G5   A5
And the parting on the left

D   A5
Is now parting on the right,

D   A5   D   E5   C/G G5
And the beards have all grown longer o - vernight.

Chorus 2

      D   A5   D   A5
I'll tip my hat to the new consti-tution,

D   A5   D   A5
Take a bow ___ for the new revo-lution.

D   A5   D   A5
Smile and grin ___ at the change all a-round,

G5   E5
Pick up my guitar and play,

G5   E5
Just like yesterday,

      G5   D
Then I'll get on my knees and pray, Yeah!

Outro

A5		G5	D	A5			G5	D	
A5		G5	D	A5			G5	D	

  Meet the new boss;   same as the old boss.

A5		D	A5		D	
A*			A5			

You Ain't Seen Nothin' Yet

Words and Music
by Randy Bachman

Melody:

I met a dev-il wom-an.

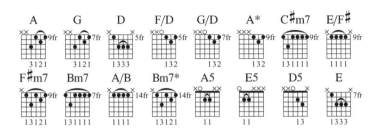

Intro   ‖: A | G   D :‖ *Play 4 times*

Verse 1

      A   G D
I met a devil woman,

      A   G D
She took my heart away.

      A   G D
She said I've had it coming to me,

      A   G D
But I wanted it that way.

Pre-Chorus 1

                    D   **F/D   G/D**
I think that   any love is good lovin'.

   A*   **C#m7**
So I took what I could get.

E/F#   **F#m7** **E/F#** **F#m7**
Mmm.   Ooh.   Ooh.

Bm7   **A/B Bm7* A/B Bm7***
  She looked at me with big brown eyes.

Chorus 1

                    A5   **N.C.**   **E5 D5 N.C.**
And said, you ain't seen nothin' yet.

                                A5   **N.C.**   **E5 D5 N.C.**
B-B-B-Baby, you just ain't ____ seen n-n-nothing yet.

                             A5   **N.C.**   **E5 D5 N.C.**
Here's something that you're never gonna forget.

                             A5   **N.C.**   **E5 D5**
B-B-B-Baby, you just ain't ____ seen n-n-nothing yet.

Nothing yet, you ain't been around.

Interlude   *Repeat Intro*

Verse 2

      A   **G D**
And now I'm feeling better,

      A   **G D**
'Cause I found out for sure.

      A   **G D**
She took me to her doctor,

      A   **G D**
And he told me I was cured.

                                  D   **F/D G/D**
Pre-Chorus 2   He said that   any love is good love.

                          A*   **C♯m7**
                  So I took what I could get.

                          E/F♯ F♯m7   **E/F♯**
                  Yes, I _____ took what I could get.

                  F♯m7   **Bm7**
                  And then she looked at me

                                          A/B Bm7* A/B Bm7*
                  With her big brown eyes.

                                  A5   **N.C.**   **E5 D5 N.C.**
Chorus 2   And said, you ain't seen nothin' yet.

                                          A5   **N.C.**   **E5   D5   N.C.**
                  B-B-B-Baby, you just ain't ____ seen n-n-nothing yet.

                                          A5   **N.C.**   **E5 D5 N.C.**
                  Here's something that you're never gonna forget.

                                          A5   **N.C.**   **E5   D5**
                  B-B-B-Baby, you just ain't ____ seen n-n-nothing yet.

                  Nothing yet. *You need educating.*

Guitar Solo | **A** | **G**   **D** |
                            Gotta go to school.
                  ‖: **A** | **G**   **D**   :‖ *Play 7 times*

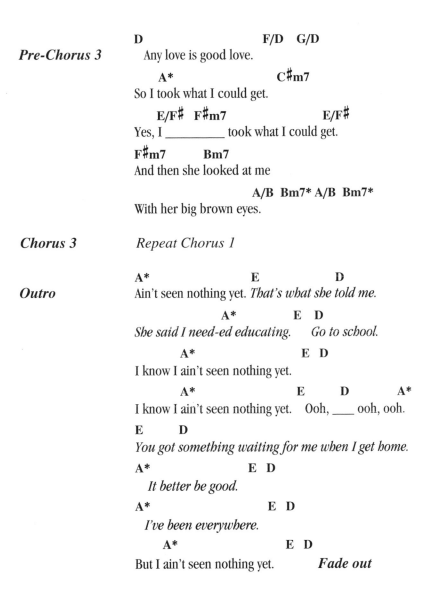

Pre-Chorus 3

D   F/D G/D
Any love is good love.

A*   C♯m7
So I took what I could get.

E/F♯ F♯m7   E/F♯
Yes, I _____ took what I could get.

F♯m7   Bm7
And then she looked at me

           A/B Bm7* A/B Bm7*
With her big brown eyes.

Chorus 3   *Repeat Chorus 1*

Outro

A*   E   D
Ain't seen nothing yet. *That's what she told me.*

        A*   E D
She said I need-ed educating. *Go to school.*

     A*   E D
I know I ain't seen nothing yet.

     A*   E   D   A*
I know I ain't seen nothing yet. Ooh, ___ ooh, ooh.

E   D
You got something waiting for me when I get home.

A*   E D
 It better be good.

A*   E D
 I've been everywhere.

     A*   E D
But I ain't seen nothing yet.   ***Fade out***

You Give Love a Bad Name

Words and Music by Desmond Child,
Jon Bon Jovi and Richie Sambora

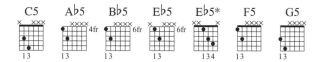

| C5 | Ab5 | Bb5 | Eb5 | Eb5* | F5 | G5 |

Intro

N.C.
Shot through the heart, and you're to blame, darlin',

You give love a bad name.

| C5 Ab5 C5 | Bb5 C5 | Ab5 Bb5 | Eb5 C5 |
| Ab5 C5 | Bb5 C5 | Ab5 Bb5 | |

Interlude 1

| N.C.(Cm) | | | Eb5* |

Verse 1

N.C.(Cm)
An angel's smile is what you sell.

You promised me heaven then put me through hell.

Chains of love got a hold of me.

When passion's a prison you can't break free.

Pre-Chorus 1	**F5** **E♭5***

Pre-Chorus 1

F5   **E♭5***
Whoa, you're a loaded gun. Yeah.

B♭5   **N.C.(B♭)**
Oh, there's nowhere to run.

No one can save me, the damage is done.

Chorus 1

C5   **A♭5 C5 B♭5**   **C5**
Shot through the heart, and you're to blame.

A♭5 **B♭5** **E♭5 C5**
You give love a bad name, bad name.

       A♭5   **C5 B♭5**   **C5**
I play my part, and you play your game.

A♭5 **B♭5** **E♭5 C5**
You give love a bad name, bad name.

    A♭5   **B♭5**
And you give love a bad name.

Interlude 2   *Repeat Interlude 1*

Verse 2

N.C.(Cm)
You paint your smile on your lips,

Blood red nails on your fingertips.

A school boy's dream, you act so shy.

Your very first kiss was your first kiss goodbye.

Pre-Chorus 2   *Repeat Pre-Chorus 1*

	C5 Ab5 C5 Bb5 C5
Chorus 2	Shot through the heart, and you're to blame.

Ab5   Bb5 Eb5 C5
You give love a bad   name, bad name.

       Ab5   C5 Bb5   C5
I play my part, and you play your game.

Ab5   Bb5 Eb5 C5
You give love a bad   name, bad name.

   Ab5   Bb5
And you give love.

Guitar Solo　| C5 Ab5 C5 | Bb5   C5 | Ab5 C5 | Bb5   C5 |

| Ab5 C5 | Bb5   C5 | Ab5 | G5 |

| | |
  Oh.

          N.C.

Chorus 3　Shot through the heart, and you're to blame.

You give love a bad name.

I play my part, and you play your game.

You give love a bad name, bad name.

C5   Ab5 C5 Bb5   C5
Shot through the heart, and you're to blame.

Ab5   Bb5 Eb5 C5
You give love a bad   name, bad name.

       Ab5   C5 Bb5   C5
I play my part, and you play your game.

Ab5   Bb5 Eb5 C5
You give love a bad   name, bad name.

   Ab5   Bb5 Eb5   C5
Outro　‖: You give love.

Ab5   Bb5 Eb5 C5
You give love.   Bad name.   :‖   *Repeat and fade*

You Shook Me All Night Long

Words and Music by Angus Young,
Malcolm Young and Brian Johnson

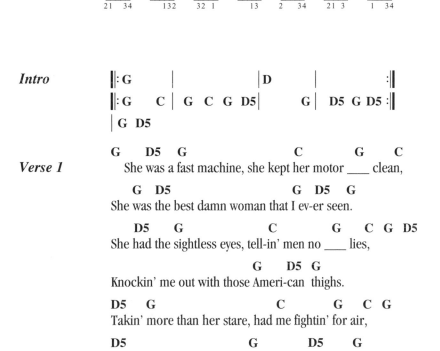

Intro

```
‖: G      |        | D    |          :‖
‖: G   C  | G  C  G  D5|     G| D5  G  D5 :‖
| G  D5
```

Verse 1

```
       G    D5  G                C        G    C
       She was a fast machine, she kept her motor ___ clean,

       G   D5                    G  D5  G
She was the best damn woman that I ev-er seen.

       D5    G              C        G    C  G  D5
She had the sightless eyes, tell-in' men no ___ lies,

                       G    D5  G
Knockin' me out with those Ameri-can  thighs.

D5   G                     C        G    C  G
Takin' more than her stare, had me fightin' for air,

D5                  G         D5     G
She told me to come, but I was alread-y there.

D5       G              C      G  C
'Cause the walls start shakin', the earth was quakin',

G  D              G        D5    G  D5
My mind was achin', and we were ___ mak - in' it.
```

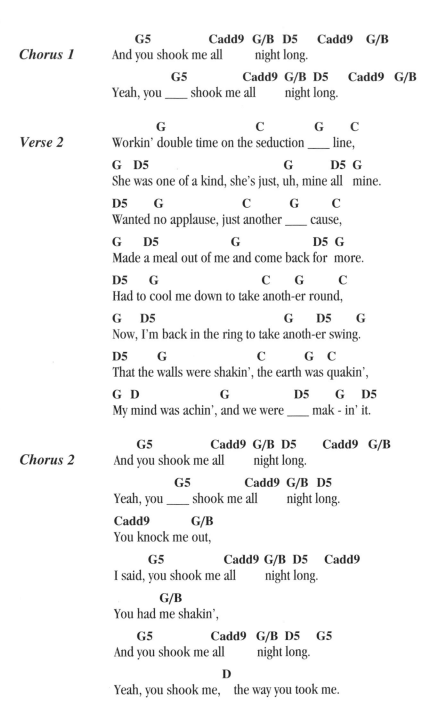

Chorus 1

```
        G5              Cadd9  G/B  D5     Cadd9   G/B
And you shook me all         night long.

              G5          Cadd9  G/B  D5    Cadd9   G/B
Yeah, you ___ shook me all        night long.
```

Verse 2

```
        G               C          G     C
Workin' double time on the seduction ___ line,

G  D5                      G         D5 G
She was one of a kind, she's just, uh, mine all  mine.

D5     G              C        G      C
Wanted no applause, just another ___ cause,

G     D5              G              D5 G
Made a meal out of me and come back for  more.

D5     G                   C     G      C
Had to cool me down to take anoth-er round,

G     D5                    G      D5    G
Now, I'm back in the ring to take anoth-er swing.

D5     G              C          G  C
That the walls were shakin', the earth was quakin',

G  D              G            D5    G   D5
My mind was achin', and we were ___ mak - in' it.
```

Chorus 2

```
        G5              Cadd9  G/B  D5     Cadd9   G/B
And you shook me all         night long.

              G5          Cadd9  G/B  D5
Yeah, you ___ shook me all        night long.

Cadd9          G/B
You knock me out,

        G5              Cadd9  G/B  D5    Cadd9
I said, you shook me all        night long.

        G/B
You had me shakin',

        G5              Cadd9  G/B  D5    G5
And you shook me all         night long.

                    D
Yeah, you shook me,    the way you took me.
```

Guitar Solo | G5   Cadd9 | G/B   D5 | Cadd9 | G/B   G5 |
                           | Cadd9 | G/B   D | Cadd9 | G/B |
                           | G5   Cadd9 | G/B   D5 | Cadd9 | G/B |
                           | G5   Cadd9 | G/B   D5 | Cadd9 | G/B |

You real-ly took me, and,

G5   **Cadd9 G/B**   **D5**   **Cadd9**

Chorus 3   You shook me all _____ night ___ long.

G/B G5   **Cadd9 G/B**   **D5**   **Cadd9**
Ah,   you shook me all _____ night ___ long.

G/B
Yeah, yeah,

    G5   **Cadd9 G/B**   **D5**   **Cadd9**
You ___ shook me all _____ night ___ long.

       G/B
You real-ly got me,

    G5   **Cadd9 G/B**   **D**   **Cadd9**
And you shook me all _____ night ___ long.

        G/B   **D**   **Cadd9**
Yeah, you shook me,

       G   **D**
Yeah, you shook me ___ all night long.

Guitar Chord Songbooks

Each book includes complete lyrics, chord symbols, and guitar chord diagrams.

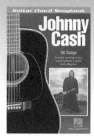   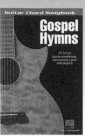 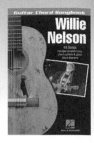

Acoustic Hits
More than 60 songs: Against the Wind • Name • One • Southern Cross • Take Me Home, Country Roads • Teardrops on My Guitar • Who'll Stop the Rain • Ziggy Stardust • and more.
00701787 ....$14.99

Acoustic Rock
80 acoustic favorites: Blackbird • Blowin' in the Wind • Layla • Maggie May • Me and Julio down by the Schoolyard • Pink Houses • and more.
00699540.................................$21.99

Alabama
50 of Alabama's best: Angels Among Us • The Closer You Get • If You're Gonna Play in Texas (You Gotta Have a Fiddle in the Band) • Mountain Music • When We Make Love • and more.
00699914.................................$14.95

The Beach Boys
59 favorites: California Girls • Don't Worry Baby • Fun, Fun, Fun • Good Vibrations • Help Me Rhonda • Wouldn't It Be Nice • dozens more!
00699566.................................$19.99

The Beatles
100 more Beatles hits: Lady Madonna • Let It Be • Ob-La-Di, Ob-La-Da • Paperback Writer • Revolution • Twist and Shout • When I'm Sixty-Four • and more.
00699562.................................$17.99

Bluegrass
Over 40 classics: Blue Moon of Kentucky • Foggy Mountain Top • High on a Mountain Top • Keep on the Sunny Side • Wabash Cannonball • The Wreck of the Old '97 • and more.
00702585.................................$14.99

Johnny Cash
58 Cash classics: A Boy Named Sue • Cry, Cry, Cry • Daddy Sang Bass • Folsom Prison Blues • I Walk the Line • RIng of Fire • Solitary Man • and more.
00699648.................................$17.99

Children's Songs
70 songs for kids: Alphabet Song • Bingo • The Candy Man • Eensy Weensy Spider • Puff the Magic Dragon • Twinkle, Twinkle Little Star • and more.
00699539.................................$16.99

Christmas Carols
80 Christmas carols: Angels We Have Heard on High • The Holly and the Ivy • I Saw Three Ships • Joy to the World • O Holy Night • and more.
00699536.................................$12.99

Christmas Songs
80 songs: All I Want for Christmas Is My Two Front Teeth • Baby, It's Cold Outside • Jingle Bell Rock • Mistletoe and Holly • Sleigh Ride • and more.
00119911.................................$14.99

Eric Clapton
75 of Slowhand's finest: I Shot the Sheriff • Knockin' on Heaven's Door • Layla • Strange Brew • Tears in Heaven • Wonderful Tonight • and more.
00699567 ....$19.99

Classic Rock
80 rock essentials: Beast of Burden • Cat Scratch Fever • Hot Blooded • Money • Rhiannon • Sweet Emotion • Walk on the Wild Side • and more.
00699598 ....$18.99

Coffeehouse Hits
57 singer-songwriter hits: Don't Know Why • Hallelujah • Meet Virginia • Steal My Kisses • Torn • Wonderwall • You Learn • and more.
00703318 ....$14.99

Country
80 country standards: Boot Scootin' Boogie • Crazy • Hey, Good Lookin' • Sixteen Tons • Through the Years • Your Cheatin' Heart • and more.
00699534 ....$17.99

Country Favorites
Over 60 songs: Achy Breaky Heart (Don't Tell My Heart) • Brand New Man • Gone Country • The Long Black Veil • Make the World Go Away • and more.
00700609 ....$14.99

Country Hits
40 classics: As Good As I Once Was • Before He Cheats • Cruise • Follow Your Arrow • God Gave Me You • The House That Built Me • Just a Kiss • Making Memories of Us • Need You Now • Your Man • and more.
00140859 ....$14.99

Country Standards
60 songs: By the Time I Get to Phoenix • El Paso • The Gambler • I Fall to Pieces • Jolene • King of the Road • Put Your Hand in the Hand • A Rainy Night in Georgia • and more.
00700608 ....$12.95

Cowboy Songs
Over 60 tunes: Back in the Saddle Again • Happy Trails • Home on the Range • Streets of Laredo • The Yellow Rose of Texas • and more.
00699636 ....$19.99

Creedence Clearwater Revival
34 CCR classics: Bad Moon Rising • Born on the Bayou • Down on the Corner • Fortunate Son • Up Around the Bend • and more.
00701786 ....$16.99

Jim Croce
37 tunes: Bad, Bad Leroy Brown • I Got a Name • I'll Have to Say I Love You in a Song • Operator (That's Not the Way It Feels) • Photographs and Memories • Time in a Bottle • You Don't Mess Around with Jim • and many more.
00148087 ....$14.99

Nirvana
40 songs: About a Girl • Come as You Are • Heart Shaped Box • The Man Who Sold the World • Smells like Teen Spirit • You Know You're Right • and more.
00699762 ....$16.99

Roy Orbison
38 songs: Blue Bayou • Oh, Pretty Woman • Only the Lonely (Know the Way I Feel) • Working for the Man • You Got It • and more.
00699752 ....$17.99

Peter, Paul & Mary
43 favorites: If I Had a Hammer (The Hammer Song) • Leaving on a Jet Plane • Puff the Magic Dragon • This Land Is Your Land • and more.
00103013...............................$19.99

Tom Petty
American Girl • Breakdown • Don't Do Me like That • Free Fallin' • Here Comes My Girl • Into the Great Wide Open • Mary Jane's Last Dance • Refugee • Runnin' Down a Dream • The Waiting • and more.
00699883 ....$15.99

Pink Floyd
30 songs: Another Brick in the Wall, Part 2 • Brain Damage • Breathe • Comfortably Numb • Hey You • Money • Mother • Run like Hell • Us and Them • Wish You Were Here • Young Lust • and many more.
00139116 ....$14.99

Pop/Rock
80 chart hits: Against All Odds • Come Sail Away • Every Breath You Take • Hurts So Good • Kokomo • More Than Words • Smooth • Summer of '69 • and more.
00699538 ....$16.99

Praise and Worship
80 favorites: Agnus Dei • He Is Exalted • I Could Sing of Your Love Forever • Lord, I Lift Your Name on High • More Precious Than Silver • Open the Eyes of My Heart • Shine, Jesus, Shine • and more.
00699634 ....$14.99

Elvis Presley
60 hits: All Shook Up • Blue Suede Shoes • Can't Help Falling in Love • Heartbreak Hotel • Hound Dog • Jailhouse Rock • Suspicious Minds • Viva Las Vegas • and more.
00699633 ....$17.99

Queen
40 hits: Bohemian Rhapsody • Crazy Little Thing Called Love • Fat Bottomed Girls • Killer Queen • Tie Your Mother Down • Under Pressure • You're My Best Friend • and more!
00702395 ....$14.99

Red Hot Chili Peppers
50 hits: Californication • Give It Away • Higher Ground • Love Rollercoaster • Scar Tissue • Suck My Kiss • Under the Bridge • and more.
00699710 ....$19.99

The Rolling Stones
35 hits: Angie • Beast of Burden • Fool to Cry • Happy • It's Only Rock 'N' Roll (But I Like It) • Miss You • Not Fade Away • Respectable • Rocks Off • Start Me Up • Time Is on My Side • Tumbling Dice • Waiting on a Friend • and more.
00137716 ....$17.99

Bob Seger
41 favorites: Against the Wind • Hollywood Nights • Katmandu • Like a Rock • Night Moves • Old Time Rock & Roll • You'll Accomp'ny Me • and more!
00701147...............................$12.99

Carly Simon
Nearly 40 classic hits, including: Anticipation • Haven't Got Time for the Pain • Jesse • Let the River Run • Nobody Does It Better • You're So Vain • and more.
00121011...............................$14.99

Sting
50 favorites from Sting and the Police: Don't Stand So Close to Me • Every Breath You Take • Fields of Gold • King of Pain • Message in a Bottle • Roxanne • and more.
00699921 ....$17.99

Taylor Swift
40 tunes: Back to December • B... Blood • Blank Space • Fearless • Fifte... • I Knew You Were Trouble • Look Wh... You Made Me Do • Love Story • Me... • Shake It Off • Speak Now • Wilde... Dreams • and many more.
00263755...............................$16.9

Three Chord Acoustic Song...
30 acoustic songs: All Apologies Blowin' in the Wind • Hold My Hand Just the Way You Are • Ring of Fire Shelter from the Storm • This Land Your Land • and more.
00123860 ....$14.

Three Chord Songs
65 includes: All Right Now • La Bam... • Lay Down Sally • Mony, Mony • Ro... Around the Clock • Rock This Town Werewolves of London • You Are ... Sunshine • and more.
00699720 ....$17.

Two-Chord Songs
Nearly 60 songs: ABC • Brick House Eleanor Rigby • Fever • Paperback Wr... er • Ramblin' Man Tulsa Time • Wh... Love Comes to Town • and more.
00119236...............................$16.

U2
40 U2 songs: Beautiful Day • Myste... ous Ways • New Year's Day • One • Su... day Bloody Sunday • Walk On • Whe... the Streets Have No Name • With ... Without You • and more.
00137744...............................$14.

Hank Williams
68 classics: Cold, Cold Heart • He... Good Lookin' • Honky Tonk Blues • I'... a Long Gone Daddy • Jambalaya (C... the Bayou) • Your Cheatin' Heart • a... more.
00700607 ....$16.

Stevie Wonder
40 of Stevie's best: For Once in My L... • Higher Ground • Isn't She Lovely • ... Cherie Amour • Sir Duke • Superstiti... • Uptight (Everything's Alright) • Yeste... Me, Yester-You, Yesterday • and more
00120862 ....$14.

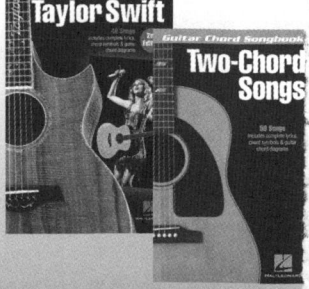

Complete contents listings available online at www.halleonard.com